Laghu Pārāsharī

An Exquisite Exposition of Vimshottari Dasha

Dr. K S Charak

UMA
PUBLICATIONS

Laghu Pārāsharī

An Exquisite Exposition of Vimshottari Dasha

First Edition : July 2020

ISBN: 978-93-817690-6-5

Price:
US$ 14.95

Published by:
UMA PUBLICATIONS
72 Gagan Vihar, New Delhi - 110051, INDIA.
Phone: +91-11-22632831
E-mail: kscharak@gmail.com

Printed by:
CreateSpace, An Amazon.com Company

PREFACE

The *Laghu Parashari* is a wonderful, condensed and concise treatise on the rules for analysis of the Vimshottari dasha of Parashara. The principles are essentially derived from the magnum opus of sage Parashara, called the *Brihat Parashara Hora Shastra.* The name Laghu Parashari is meant to convey that it is the smaller classic of the sage, to distinguish it from the bigger classic, the BPHS. The author is unknown but is most certainly some extremely brilliant and accomplished practitioner of Vedic astrology, well versed in the Parashari system. He seems to have himself kept his name a secret, a paragon of self-effacement! He has given the name '*Ududaaya Pradeepa*' to this composition, meaning a treatise that shines light on the nakshatra-based dasha of Parashara. He hastens to add that the principles apply only to the Vimshottari dasha of Parashara and to no other nakshatra-based dasha.

This classic lays emphasis on recognising grahas which are functional benefics and functional malefics, the (yoga-) karakas and marakas, and then identifying the various yogas which the different grahas form. The yogas in their unblemished form give highly benevolent results while those which are blemished by adverse house lordship prove to be less effective in yielding good results. The static promise inherent in the chart, indicated by the various yogas, finds fruition when the dynamic factor of appropriate dashas comes into operation. Extremely subtle and refined principles of dasha interpretation find mention in this classic. This classic only contains yogas which are based on the lordship of different houses and does not mention scores of other yogas which are formed by specific disposition of different grahas independent of their house lordship. This is not to say that those yogas are not important. The author makes it clear in the very beginning that basic material not included in this classic may be learnt from other standard books on astrology. Principles about the determination of longevity and the dashas indicating the time of death are relevant as far as the feasibility of reaping the effects of the yogas during the lifetime of the native is concerned.

It is important to realise that this classic explains the operation of dashas in a manner that no other available classic does. The shlokas in the body of the text not only contain rich astrological material but also indicate the excellence of the Sanskrit language wherein brevity conceals vastness. A wealth of astrological wisdom lies enshrined in a mere forty-two verses. Some of the shlokas are liable to multiple interpretations and a very careful attention has to be paid to the construction of each verse and the meaning it conveys.

Almost all the shlokas in the Laghu Parashari find place in the popular south Indian classic, the *Jataka Chandrika,* which additionally contains material regarding the principles of matching of charts for the purpose of marriage. Another popular classic on astrology, the *Phaladeepika* of Mantreshwara, picks up twelve shlokas from the *Laghu Parashari* to include in its chapter on dasha interpretation (Ch. 20; shlokas 43 to 54). Savants of astrology agree that this small classic contains profound principles of dasha interpretation which no serious student of astrology can afford to ignore.

This translation of and commentary on the *Laghu Parashari* has been prepared with the intention to provide rich and authentic material on Vedic astrology to the

English-knowing seeker of astrological wisdom. All shlokas have been thoroughly explained and numerous examples of known individuals have been provided in order to elucidate the principles.

In the interpretation of the Sanskrit text, we have taken the help and guidance of Dr. Suresh Chandra Mishra, an accomplished Sanskrit scholar and author. Our friend from USA, Christine Fournier, a Vedic astrologer herself, took up the burden of subediting this text. Rajeev Jhanji gave shape to my typed text and Vinay Aditya designed the cover page. Yashwant Rawat as usual has done a great job inserting the horoscopic charts and carrying out numerous small but significant corrections and modifications where indicated. I remain beholden to all these friends of mine.

Dr. K S Charak

Senior Consultant & Chief
of General Surgery,
Indian Spinal Injuries Centre,
Vasant Kunj,
New Delhi-110070 (India)

June 11, 2020

CONTENTS

CHAPTER 1

संज्ञाध्यायः
The Basics

सिद्धान्तमौपनिषदं शुद्धान्तं परमेष्ठिनः ।
शोणाधरं महः किंचिद् वीणाधरमुपास्महे ॥ 1 ॥

1. We offer our worship to goddess Saraswati, of red lips, the blazing light (of knowledge), the essence of the Upanishadas, holding Veena in hands, and residing in the heart of Lord Brahma.

Comments: It is customary to offer worship to an appropriate deity before undertaking any auspicious venture. Goddess Saraswati, the goddess of knowledge and wisdom, is the natural choice for prayers by astrologers and spiritual seekers. It was during the early days of Creation that lord Brahma, the Creator, gave origin to several beings and species either through a mental process of deep meditation or from out of His own body. Goddess Saraswati was born of Lord Brahma's face. Having originated from Brahma's body, she happens to be His daughter and remains very close to His heart.

As Lord Brahma went into deep meditation, there happened an excessive flow of sattvaguna, the sublime quality, which took the form of a girl. This was Saraswati, the daughter of Lord Brahma. Lord Brahma immediately took a liking for her and bade her to assume three forms in order to fulfill three functions. Said He, "Reside, through your one form, on everybody's tongue and especially dance on the tongues of the learned and the wise; through another form of yours, do descend to the earth and be a sacred river, to wash off the sins of the earthlings; and through a third form, continue to reside in My heart."

The above shloka (verse) does not actually mention the name of goddess Saraswati. However, the qualities of the deity for worship mentioned in it all belong to goddess Saraswati. It mentions of an incarnate effulgence or blaze of light which has some sort of a superhuman form, which has a red lower lip, and which holds the Veena, goddess Saraswati's musical instrument, in its hands. This incarnate effulgence represents the extract or essence of the Upanishadas, which embody the Vedic wisdom, and resides in the heart of Lord Brahma. The Puranas say that chanting of the mantras extolling goddess Saraswati for only one month can convert an ignoramus into an intellectual. We who seek astrological wisdom offer our worship to mother Saraswati. May she, dancing on our tongues, make us utter only truth.

वयं पाराशरीं होरामनुसृत्य यथामति ।
उडुदायप्रदीपाख्यं कुर्मो दैवविदां मुदे ॥ 2 ॥

2. We present, for the pleasure of the erudite, the text named the 'Ududaaya Pradeepa', according to our understanding of the Hora Shaastra of Parashara.

Comments: The word 'Udu' means nakshatra, one of the twenty-seven clusters of stars which adorn the zodiac; 'Daaya' means dasha or an operational period of a graha or 'planet' which is used to time the events according to Vedic astrology. 'Ududaaya Pradeepa' thus means the 'text that elucidates the results of the nakshatra dasha'. To differentiate it from sage Parashara's magnum opus, the *Brihat Parashara Hora Shaastra (BPHS)*, this text is conveniently called the *Laghu Parashari*, the smaller text of Parashara. The purpose of presenting this text, we are told, is to provide pleasure to the erudite. The pleasure for the erudite lies in subjects which are lofty in substance. This small text is thus designed to provide rich astrological material and guidance to the scholarly and the knowledgeable. One must possess an understanding of astrological principles to be able to follow the canons mentioned so tersely in the body of this text.

Well laid down principles of sage Parashara form the basis of the dicta here. The subject is the nakshatra dasha of Parashara. Sage Parashara does not mention only one dasha system in the *Brihat Parashara Hora Shaastra*. And the Parashari dashas are nakshatra based only. So it has to be just one of the several Parashari dashas which must be the subject matter of this small classic. The next shloka clarifies this.

फलानि नक्षत्रदशाप्रकारेण विवृण्महे ।
दशा विंशोत्तरी चात्र ग्राह्या नाष्टोत्तरी मता ॥ 3 ॥

3. We shall explain the results according to the nakshatra dasha. In this text, only the Vimshottari dahsa is acceptable; the Ashtottari is not acceptable.

Comments: The Ashtottari is one of the several nakshatra based dashas of Parashara. This popular dasha system covers a time span of one hundred and eight years.

However, the author of the *'Laghu Parashari'* clarifies that the principles to be enunciated hereafter would apply only to the Vimshottari dasha and not to the Ashtottari (or any other nakshatra based) dasha.

The Grahas: Vedic astrology recognizes nine grahas (often loosely translated as 'planets' for want of an accurate descriptive word) or heavenly 'bodies' which happen to indicate terrestrial events according to their astronomical disposition at any given moment of time. These are the Sun, the Moon, Mars, Mercury, Jupiter, Venus, Saturn, Rahu and Ketu. Whereas the Sun and the Moon are considered the luminaries (one a star and the other a satellite), the next five (Mars to Saturn) are planets, and the last two (Rahu and Ketu) are just mathematical points without a physical body. A horoscope is the mapping of the astronomical position of the grahas at any given moment of time. The horoscope erected for the time of birth of an individual throws light on the promise that life holds for that individual. This is the static promise. The dynamic aspect of this is provided by the study of the dashas.

Relevance of Dasha: The study of dashas, or operational periods of grahas, is necessary to determine the time when the promise inherent in the horoscope could fructify. Each graha is allotted a certain time span during which it dominates the events in the life of an individual. This, along with the Gochara or planetary transits, constitutes the dynamic aspect of horoscopic study. An understanding of both the static promise in the horoscope and the time of unfolding of that promise are important aspects of Vedic astrology. The Vimshottari dasha, the subject matter of this classic, as the name suggests, covers a time span of one hundred and twenty years. This time span has been allotted, in a very specific manner, amongst the nine grahas mentioned above. Also, the order in which these dasha periods operate is highly specific. Of paramount importance is the location of the Moon in the zodiac at the time of birth. Position of the Moon determines the graha which will have its first dasha operating in the life of an individual, and the duration of that dasha.

Relevance of Nakshatras: The whole zodiac of 360 degrees is equally divided into twenty-seven parts, each called a nakshatra and having a span of 13°20' arc. These twenty-seven nakshatras are allotted to the nine grahas so that each graha owns three nakshatras. For determining the dasha operating at the time of birth of a native, one has to find the nakshatra in the zodiac where the Moon is located at the time of birth. The lord of that nakshatra would be the graha which would run its dasha at the time of birth. The order of Vimshottari dasha starting from the Sun is as follows: Sun, Moon, Mars, Rahu, Jupiter, Saturn, Mercury, Ketu and Venus. After the first dasha, the subsequent dashas would follow in the order mentioned. The first nakshatra that belongs to the Sun is Krittika. Thus grahas own the nakshatras starting from Krittika by the Sun, Rohini by the Moon and so on, till they complete three cycles. The following table (**Table 1**) gives the order of the Vimshottari dasha, the nakshatras owned by the grahas and the duration in years of their dasha periods.

Vimshottari dasha – Finer Divisions: The periods mentioned against each graha indicate the dasha duration of these grahas in years. These are their major periods, also called the Mahadasha (MD). Thus, the Sun has an MD of six years, the Moon of ten years, Mars of seven years and so on. The full span of the nakshatra in the zodiac, an arc of 13°20', represents the dasha duration of the graha that owns that nakshatra. From the exact location of the Moon in a given nakshatra, one can find out how much of the span of that nakshatra has been already traversed by the

Table 1:
Nakshatras, dasha lords and duration of Vimshottari dasha.

N A K S H A T R A S			*Dasha Lord*	*Duration of Dasha*
Krittika	U. Phalguni	U. Ashadha	Sun	6 years
Rohini	Hasta	Shravana	Moon	10 years
Mrigashira	Chitra	Dhanishtha	Mars	7 years
Ardra	Swati	Shatabhishaj	Rahu	18 years
Punarvasu	Vishakha	P. Bhadrapada	Jupiter	16 years
Pushya	Anuradha	U. Bhadrapada	Saturn	19 years
Ashlesha	Jyeshtha	Revati	Mercury	17 years
Magha	Moola	Ashwini	Ketu	7 years
P. Phalguni	P. Ashadha	Bharani	Venus	20 years

Moon and how much remains to be traversed. The span of nakshatra that remains to be traversed by the Moon indicates the balance of dasha of the graha that owns that nakshatra. For example, if the Moon at birth is located in the middle of the nakshatra Bharani belonging to Venus, it has already traversed half the nakshatra and has yet to traverse another half. The complete nakshatra of Venus indicates twenty years of dasha period. So if at the time of birth the Moon is in the middle of Venus' nakshatra, ten years of Venus dasha is already past and a balance of ten years remains at birth. So the native would run ten years of Venus dasha at birth and that would be followed by six years of Sun dasha, followed by ten years of Moon dasha, and so on. These are the MD's.

Since an MD is a period of long duration, each dasha is further divided into sub-periods. These sub-periods are called as Antardashas (AD's). The MD of each graha will havc its duration subdivided into nine parts, belonging to each of the nine grahas, in the same proportion in which each graha has its MD. Thus the MD of any given graha will have the AD's of all the other grahas, also in the same order as the Vimshottari dasha order, starting from its own AD as the first AD in its MD. For further closer timing of events, each AD is further subdivided in sub-sub-periods called the Pratyantardasha (PD). Each AD would have the PD of each of the nine grahas, its own PD running as the first PD and the remaining PD's following in the same Vimshottari dasha order. The PD's can be further subdivided into finer divisions, the fourth order being called the Sookshma dasha and the fifth order being called the Praana dasha. In general, most of the astrological work can be accomplished by using MD, AD and PD.

There are numerous methods in which the dashas need to be interpreted. The simplest method is to consider the dasha lords from the lagna. Sage Parashara, however, recommends considering dasha lordship from the Moon and the Sun also. The sage also recommends that the MD lord may be considered as the lagna so that the AD lordship is considered not only from the lagna but also from the MD lord.

Gochara or Transits: The text under consideration mentions about the various yogas and the use of dashas to pinpoint the events that may occur during the lifetime of a native. However, an important consideration which is essential for making any correct prediction is the recognition of the transit of grahas at the time of a likely event. While the horoscope provides a fixed picture of the astronomical position of grahas at the time of birth, the continuous movement of the grahas in the zodiac goes on, activating different areas of the horoscope and precipitating events according to the operation of the dashas. While the dashas point to the likely time of an event, it is the transiting grahas that ensure their precipitation. Very often, when an appropriate dasha indicating a certain event is in operation, the transits at that time are also favourable for that event. However, if a dasha indicates a certain event and the transits at that time indicate otherwise, the event is unlikely to happen. That becomes one reason for failed predictions. While the subject of 'gochara' or transits is outside the scope of the present treatise, the reader is well advised to take into consideration the transits of grahas at the time of operating dashas to increase his rate of successful predictions.

बुधैर्भावादयः सर्वे ज्ञेयाः सामान्यशास्त्रतः ।
एतच्छास्त्रानुसारेण संज्ञां ब्रूमो विशेषतः ॥ 4 ॥

4. The wise should obtain the knowledge of the houses, etc., from other standard texts. Here, we shall deal with special subjects according to the Shaastra.

Comments: The author here does not want to go into the basic astrological principles which he expects the student to learn from the standard, available, popular texts on the subject. He would only confine himself to the special areas of this subject. We would, however, like to very briefly touch on some of the important basic principles of this subject, especially about the components of the horoscope, which the student must arm himself with before proceeding further.

Houses: A horoscope is a chart of the astronomical positions of grahas at a given moment of time. The body of the horoscope consists of twelve houses which rule over all the conceivable aspects of an individual's life. The first house is called the lagna or the ascendant and is supposed to be the most important house of the horoscope. The grahas indicate their results depending on the nature of the lagna. In other words, the grahas are subservient to the lagna. Briefly, the twelve houses indicate the following:

First house (Lagna): Physical health, wealth, body, strength, longevity, head, brain, social stature, fame, character;

Second house: Finances, speech, inclinations, food, taste, immediate family members, eyes, vision, teeth, tongue, oral cavity;

Third house: Siblings, courage, physical fitness, hobbies, talent, longevity of parents, sports, neighbourhood, dreams, ears, hearing, neck, longevity;

Fourth house: Home, mother, lands, houses, farming, comforts at home, vehicles, chest, lungs, breast, heart;

Fifth house: Progeny, learning, thinking, higher education, scholarship, fascinations, discrimination, speculation, heart, upper abdomen, liver, gall bladder, pregnancy;

Sixth house: Enemy, disease, accidents, injury, wounds, theft, loans, debts, quarrels, imprisonment, pets, servants, intestines, appendix, kidneys, tuberculosis, poisoning;

Seventh house: Spouse, sexual partner, marriage, adultery, lust or passion, sexual union, love affairs, business partners, attainment of status, lower urinary tract, prostate;

Eighth house: Longevity, death, obstacles, defeat, disconti nuity, sin, killing a living being, nature or place of death, amputation, external genitalia, wickedness, intrigues, scandals, inheritance, hidden treasure;

Ninth house: Dharma; virtuous deeds, pilgrimage, religious inclination, destiny, father, preceptor, spiritual inclination, long journey, hips, thighs;

Tenth house: Karma, vocation, source of livelihood, government service, high status, royal honours, political power, knee joint;

Eleventh house: Gains, earning, acquisitions, fulfilment of desires, longevity of mother, rewards, recognition, achievements, proficiency, legs, recovery from illness;

Twelfth house: Expenditure, loss of wealth, pleasures of the bed, loss of authority, distant travel, foreign lands, secret learning, emancipation, loss of sleep, hospitalization, mental imbalance, feet, death.

One needs to know further about the houses. They can be classed as follows:

Kendras:	Houses 1, 4, 7 and 10;
Panapharas:	Houses 2, 5, 8 and 11;
Apoklimas:	Houses 3, 6, 9 and 12;
Trikonas:	Houses 1, 5 and 9;
Upachayas:	Houses 3, 6, 10 and 11;
Trika houses:	Houses 6, 8 and 12.

Rashis or Signs: The zodiac of 360 degrees is subdivided into twelve rashis or signs. Each rashi is an arc of 30 degrees on the zodiac. The names of the rashis, their English equivalents, their extent in the zodiac and their symbols are shown in **table 2.**

The rashi rising on the eastern horizon at a given moment of time is called the lagna or ascendant, and indicates the first house of the horoscope. These rashis have their own special characteristics which are important in prediction. Some of the important characteristics of rashis are being given here:

Table 2: Rashis, their extent and their symbols.

	Rashis	*English Name*	*Extent*	*Symbol*
1.	Mesha	Aries	0° – 30°	♈
2.	Vrisha	Taurus	30° – 60°	♉
3.	Mithuna	Gemini	60° – 90°	♊
4.	Karka	Cancer	90° – 120°	♋
5.	Simha	Leo	120° – 150°	♌
6.	Kanya	Virgo	150° – 180°	♍
7.	Tula	Libra	180° – 210°	♎
8.	Vrishchika	Scorpio	210° – 240°	♏
9.	Dhanu	Sagittarius	240° – 270°	♐
10.	Makara	Capricorn	270° – 300°	♑
11.	Kumbha	Aquarius	300° – 330°	♒
12.	Meena	Pisces	330° – 360°	♓

Gender:

Male: Odd rashis – 1, 3, 5, 7, 9 and 11;
Female: Even rashis – 2, 4, 6, 8, 10 and 12.

Benefic or otherwise:

Malefic: Odd rashis – 1, 3, 5, 7, 9 and 11;
Benefic: Even rashis – 2, 4, 6, 8, 10 and 12.

Movable or otherwise:

Chara/Movable: Rashis 1, 4, 7 and 10;
Sthira/Fixed: Rashis 2, 5, 8 and 11;
Dwiswabhava/Mutable: Rashis 3, 6, 9 and 12.

Directions:

East: Rashis 1, 5 and 9;
South: Rashis 2, 6 and 10;
West: Rashis 3, 7 and 11;
North: Rashis 4, 8 and 12.

Inherent nature:

Fiery: Rashis 1, 5 and 9;
Eathy: Rashis 2, 6 and 10;
Airy: Rashis 3, 7 and 11;
Watery: Rashis 4, 8 and 12.

Biological characters:

Quadruped (Chatushpada):
Rashis 1, 2, 5, posterior half of 9, and anterior half of 10;

Biped (Dwipada):
Rashis 3, 6, 7, 11 and anterior half of 9;

Insect (Keeta):
Rashis 4 and 8;

Inhabiting water (Jalachara):
Rashis 12 and posterior half of 10.

Nature of rising:

Sheershodaya (rising by the head):
Rashis 3, 5, 6, 7, 8 and 11;

Prishtodaya (rising by the hind side):
Rashis 1, 2, 4, 9 and 10;

Ubhayodaya (rising by the head and tail):
Rashi 12.

Lords:

The twelve rashis, from Mesha to Meena, are owned respectively by Mars, Venus, Mercury, Moon, Sun, Mercury, Venus, Mars, Jupiter, Saturn, Saturn and Jupiter.

Grahas

Vedic astrology recognizes nine grahas, from the Sun to Ketu (**Table 3**). The horoscope consists of a charting of the twelve rashis starting with the lagna, or the rashi rising

Table 3: Grahas, their English equivalents and their symbols.

Vedic Name	*English Equivalent*	*Symbol*
Ravi (Surya)	Sun	☉
Chandra	Moon	☽
Mangala	Mars	♂
Budha	Mercury	☿
Guru (Brihaspati)	Jupiter	♃
Shukra	Venus	♀
Shani	Saturn	♄
Rahu (Dragon's head)	Moon's ascending node	☊
Ketu (Dragon's tail)	Moon's decending node	☋

at the eastern horizon at the time of birth, as the first house and locating the grahas therein depending upon the astronomical position of grahas at that time. The inherent characteristics of grahas are important in predictive astrology.

Important considerations about grahas

The grahas give results according to their inherent characteristics, their location, their strength or weakness, their associations, and whether they are retrograde or combust or otherwise. The specific mutual dispositions of grahas give rise to several yogas which modify their results for better or worse depending on the nature of their interactions. Some of the inherent characteristics of the grahas are being described here.

Lordship over rashis

The seven grahas, from the Sun to Saturn rule over the twelve rashis so that the Sun and the Moon own one rashi each while the remaining five grahas own two rashis each. Rahu and Ketu, having no physical existence, are generally not thought to rule over any sign. The grahas rule over the twelve rashis as follows:

The Sun	rules over	Simha;
The Moon	rules over	Karka;
Mars	rules over	Mesha and Vrishchika;
Mercury	rules over	Mithuna and Kanya;
Jupiter	rules over	Dhanu and Meena;
Venus	rules over	Vrisha and Tula; and
Saturn	rules over	Makara and Kumbha.

Essential nature

Sattvika (good and noble):	Sun, Moon, Jupiter;
Rajasika (active and just):	Mercury, Venus;
Tamasika (dark and base):	Mars, Saturn.

Social status

King:	Sun and Moon;
Commander-in-Chief:	Mars;
Heir apparent:	Mercury;
Ministers:	Jupiter and Venus;
Servant:	Saturn;
Army:	Rahu and Ketu.

Benefics and Malefics

Natural benefics:	Moon, Mercury, Jupiter, Venus;
Natural malefics:	Sun, Mars, Saturn, Rahu, Ketu. An ill-associated Mercury and a weak Moon also tend to behave as malefics.

Exaltation, debilitation and Moola-Trikona

Grahas are strong and favourable when placed in their own houses or in their exaltation or in their Moola-Trikona signs. Exactly six signs away from their exaltation point is the debilitation point of the grahas. See **Table 4**.

Table 4: Exaltation, debilitation and Moola-Trikona of grahas.

Planet	*Exaltation*	*Debilitation*	*Mooltrikona*
The Sun	Aries 10°	Libra 10°	Leo 0°-20°
The Moon	Taurus 3°	Scorpio 3°	Taurus 4°-20°
Mars	Capricorn 28°	Cancer 28°	Aries 0°-12°
Mercury	Virgo 15°	Pisces 15°	Virgo 16°-20°
Jupiter	Cancer 5°	Capricorn 5°	Sagittarius 0°-10°
Venus	Pisces 27°	Virgo 27°	Libra 0°-15°
Saturn	Libra 20°	Aries 20°	Aquarius 0°-20°

Natural mutual relationship of grahas:

Grahas are naturally disposed as friends, enemies or equals toward other grahas. A graha's friends are its exaltation sign lord and the grahas that own houses 2, 12, 5, 9, 4 and 8 from its Moola-Trikona sign. **Table 5** shows the natural mutual relationship of grahas according to the above principle.

Table 5: Natural mutual relationship of grahas.

Planet	*Friends*	*Enemies*	*Neutrals*
The Sun	Mon, Mar, Jup	Ven, Sat	Mer
The Moon	Sun, Mer	–	Mar, Jup, Ven, Sat
Mars	Sun, Mon, Jup	Mer	Ven, Sat
Mercury	Sun, Ven	Mon	Mar, Jup, Sat
Jupiter	Sun, Mon, Mar	Mer, Ven	Sat
Venus	Mer, Sat	Sun, Mon	Mar, Jup
Saturn	Mer, Ven	Sun, Mon, Mar	Jup

Combustion and retrogression:

Grahas that get too close to the Sun lose their lustre, their strength and their benevolence. They are labeled as combust. Their distances from the Sun when they become combust are as follows:

Moon:	within 12° of the Sun;
Mars:	within 17° of the Sun;
Mercury:	within 14° of the Sun (within 12° if retrograde);
Jupiter:	within 11° of the Sun;
Venus:	within 10° of the Sun (within 8° if retrograde);
Saturn:	within 15° of the Sun.

Grahas also sometimes appear to be moving in the reverse direction in the zodiac instead their usual west to east movement. Such grahas are called retrograde. The Sun and the Moon do not become retrograde while Rahu and Ketu are (almost) always retrograde. A retrograde graha tends to produce unexpected results and is generally adverse for health.

Yogas

Grahas yield results in accordance with their disposition in the chart. Specific dispositions of grahas, generally in combination but sometimes alone, tend to yield specific results. Specific dispositions of grahas that yield specific results are called yogas. In the *Laghu Parashari*, the yogas that are mentioned depend upon the house lordship of grahas. However, there are numerous yogas that are independent of house lordship. They produce their results as described in the classics but the results eventually do get modified by the house lordship of their constituent grahas. No study of a horoscope can be considered complete without analyzing prominent yogas present therein. A few of those yogas need to be mentioned here.

Pancha-Mahapurusha yogas

Grahas from Mars to Saturn, by their location in kendras identical with their own rashi or rashi of exaltation lead to five potent rajayogas. These go by the names Ruchaka, Bhadra, Hamsa, Malavya and Shasha respectively for grahas from Mars to Saturn. Five prominent personalities or categories of individuals result from these, endowed with enhanced qualities of the grahas which cause them. These qualities for grahas from Mars to Saturn respectively are courage and strength, intelligence, knowledge and wisdom, art and beauty, and leadership over the masses.

Gaja-Kesari yoga

When Jupiter occupies a kendra from the Moon and is additionally associated with or aspected by benefics, and is neither debilitated nor combust, a very powerful yoga called the Gaja-Kesari results. This yoga confers on the native lasting renown, wealth, wisdom, noble qualities and success over others. The native gains a status equivalent to that of a king. While the Gaja-Kesari yoga is a powerful yoga, the status of its constituents and their lordship should be examined well. Excellent results are experienced when the Moon and Jupiter are strong, own good houses and occupy good houses like the kendras and trikonas. This yoga is of common occurrence. Hence it must be analysed very carefully to avoid pitfalls in prediction.

Kartari yogas

When a house or a house lord is surrounded by grahas in both adjacent houses, a Kartari ('scissors') yoga results. It is called a Shubha-Kartari if the surrounding grahas are natural benefics, and a Paapa-Kartari if the surrounding grahas are natural malefics. A Paapa-Kartari around the lagna imparts to the native criminal tendencies, ill health and impure food. Paapa-Kartari yoga around any graha markedly restricts the function of that graha. A Paapa-Kartari is more intense if the malefic in the preceding house is direct and the one in the succeedinghouse is retrograde.

Neecha-Bhanga rajayoga

A neecha graha is the one which is debilitated. A graha in debilitation does not have strength to deliver its results.

Before attributing the likely results to a debilitated graha, it is important to identify any cancellation of debilitation in the chart.

A graha achieves Neecha-Bhanga when:

(a) The lord of the house where a graha is debilitated (i.e., the debilitation lord of the graha) is in a kendra from the lagna or the Moon;

(b) The exaltation lord of the debilitated graha is in a kendra from the lagna or the Moon;

(c) The debilitated graha is associated with or aspeted by it debilitation lord;

(d) The debilitated graha is associated with or aspected by its exaltation lord;

(e) The exaltation and debilitation lords of the graha are mutually related by conjunction, aspect or exchange of houses (see later, under shloka 14);

(f) The debilitated graha exchanges houses with its debilitation lord; and

(g) Two debilitated grahas aspect each other.

A neecha graha, because of its inherent weakness, gives adverse results during its dasha. When a Neecha-Bhanga yoga is present, the debilitation yields place to a benefic rajayoga productive of favourable results.

Nakshatras

While the zodiac is divided into twelve equal parts called the rashis, each a span of 30°, it is also divided into twenty-seven parts called the nakshatras. It is necessary to have an understanding of how the nakshatras are related to the rashis on the zodiac. **Table 6** gives an idea about the interrelationship among the rashis, the nakshatras and the nakshatra lords.

Table 6: Rashis, nakshatras and nakshatra lords.

	Rashis		*Nakshatra*	*Extent* *s*	*d*	*m*	*Pada*	*Lord*
1.	Mesha (Aries)	1.	Ashvini	0	13	20	4	Ketu
		2.	Bharani	0	26	40	4	Venus
		3.	Krittika	1	0	0	1	Sun
2.	Vrisha (Taurus)	3.	Krittika	1	10	0	3	Sun
		4.	Rohini	1	23	20	4	Moon
		5.	Mrigashira	2	0	0	2	Mars
3.	Mithuna (Gemini)	5.	Mrigashira	2	6	40	2	Mars
		6.	Ardra	2	20	0	4	Rahu
		7.	Punarvasu	3	0	0	3	Jupiter
4.	Karka (Cancer)	7.	Punarvasu	3	3	20	1	Jupiter
		8.	Pushya	3	16	40	4	Saturn
		9.	Ashlesha	4	0	0	4	Mercury
5.	Simha (Leo)	10.	Magha	4	13	20	4	Ketu
		11.	Purva Phalguni	4	26	40	4	Venus
		12.	Uttara Phalguni	5	0	0	1	Sun
6.	Kanya (Virgo)	12.	Uttara Phalguni	5	10	0	3	Sun
		13.	Hasta	5	23	20	4	Moon
		14.	Chitra	6	0	0	2	Mars
7.	Tula (Libra)	14.	Chitra	6	6	40	2	Mars
		15.	Swati	6	20	0	4	Rahu
		16.	Vishakha	7	0	0	3	Jupiter
8.	Vrishchika (Scorpio)	16.	Vishakha	7	3	20	1	Jupiter
		17.	Anuradha	7	16	40	4	Saturn
		18.	Jyeshtha	8	0	0	4	Mercury
9.	Dhanu (Sagitta-rius)	19.	Moola	8	13	20	4	Ketu
		20.	Purva Ashadha	8	26	40	4	Venus
		21.	Uttara Ashadha	9	0	0	1	Sun
10.	Makara (Capricorn)	21.	Uttara Ashadha	9	10	0	3	Sun
		22.	Shravana	9	23	20	4	Moon
		23.	Dhanishtha	10	0	0	2	Mars
11.	Kumbha (Aquarius)	23.	Dhanishtha	10	6	40	2	Mars
		24.	Shatabhisha	10	20	0	4	Rahu
		25.	P. Bhadrapada	11	0	0	3	Jupiter
12.	Meena (Pisces)	25.	P. Bhadrapada	11	3	20	1	Jupiter
		26.	U. Bhadrapada	11	16	40	4	Saturn
		27.	Revati	12	0	0	4	Mercury

The Vargas

Vargas are the subdivisions of a rashi. One rashi is an arc of 30 degrees. Since the zodiac appears to go around the earth once in twenty-four hours, it means that all the twelve rashis appear to go around the earth once in twenty-four hours. Since the earth rotates in a west-to-east direction, the twelve rashis appear to circulate around the earth in an east-to-west direction. Each rashi that appears on the eastern horizon thus takes a certain amount of time to rise completely, and is followed by the next rashi that takes its own time to rise on the eastern horizon, and this goes on. Since twelve rashis take twenty-four hours to complete one circle around the earth, it is logical to consider that the average time a rashi takes to rise will be some two hours, varying by a few or several minutes depending upon the nature of the rashi and the degree of latitude of the place where a native is located. Since the rashi rising at the eastern horizon is the lagna or the first house of the horoscope, it means that several natives taking birth during a time span of roughly two hours would have the same lagna. In other words, they would have the same horoscopes. This would make differentiation between individuals born close in time difficult. To overcome this handicap, the rishis advocated the divisions of rashis, called the vargas. Sage Parashara has advocated sixteen special divisions or vargas. Obviously, to use all the finer divisions, one would need to record an accurate time of birth and calculate the positions of lagna and grahas very accurately. In practice, most astrologers confine themselves to six or seven vargas (Shadvargas or Saptavargas).

The *Laghu Parashari* refers only to the rashi chart or the lagna kundali. It does not mention the varga charts.

However, the recommendation for learning the basics from other standard or popular texts only means that one should not ignore this important aspect of Vedic astrology. Many astrologers do not want to go into even the six or the seven vargas. It has been suggested by the authorities on the subject that no horoscope (rashi chart) should be analysed without simultaneously studying the navamsha chart (based on the ninth division of a rashi). Authorities have gone thus far to say that the navamsha takes precedence over the rashi chart should there be a conflict between the two. We completely agree with this concept. However, we also advocate the use of the dashamsha chart (based on tenth division of a rashi) along with the navamsha. There are nine navamshas in a rashi so that each navamsha is an arc of 3°20'. Similarly, there are ten dashamshas in each rashi so that one dashamsha is an arc of 3 degrees. While the navamsha chart, like the rashi chart, is relevant to all aspects of life, and more, the dashamsha chart primarily deals with the Karma and the vocation of the individual. In the present day circumstances, it appears to us that the Karma takes a significant position in the life of the modern individual. It is also especially relevant to the principles of the *Laghu Parashari* which mainly deals with important yogas and yogakarakas so important for one's profession and Karma. Hence a dashamsha chart too must be studied along with the rashi chart and the navamsha chart. **Tables 7 and 8** indicate the navamshas and dashamshas for various rashis/lagnas.

In addition to the above, we would recommend the drekkana chart to be included along with rashi and navamsha for charts where medical problems are to be studied. Drekkana is one-third of a rashi and is an arc

Table 7: The navamsha chart.

	SIGNS											
Navamsha	**1**	**2**	**3**	**4**	**5**	**6**	**7**	**8**	**9**	**10**	**11**	**12**
1. 3°20'	1	10	7	4	1	10	7	4	1	10	7	4
2. 6°40'	2	11	8	5	2	11	8	5	2	11	8	5
3. 10°00'	3	12	9	6	3	12	9	6	3	12	9	6
4. 13°20'	4	1	10	7	4	1	10	7	4	1	10	7
5. 16°40'	5	2	11	8	5	2	11	8	5	2	11	8
6. 20°00'	6	3	12	9	6	3	12	9	6	3	12	9
7. 23°20'	7	4	1	10	7	4	1	10	7	4	1	10
8. 26°40'	8	5	2	11	8	5	2	11	8	5	2	11
9. 30°00'	9	6	3	12	9	6	3	12	9	6	3	12

Table 8: The dashamsha chart.

	SIGNS											
Dashamsha	**1**	**2**	**3**	**4**	**5**	**6**	**7**	**8**	**9**	**10**	**11**	**12**
1. 0°-3°	1	10	3	12	5	2	7	4	9	6	11	8
2. 3°-6°	2	11	4	1	6	3	8	5	10	7	12	9
3. 6°-9°	3	12	5	2	7	4	9	6	11	8	1	10
4. 9°-12°	4	1	6	3	8	5	10	7	12	9	2	11
5. 12°-15°	5	2	7	4	9	6	11	8	1	10	3	12
6. 15°-18°	6	3	8	5	10	7	12	9	2	11	4	1
7. 18°-21°	7	4	9	6	11	8	1	10	3	12	5	2
8. 21°-24°	8	5	10	7	12	9	2	11	4	1	6	3
9. 24°-27°	9	6	11	8	1	10	3	12	5	2	7	4
10. 27°-30°	10	7	12	9	2	11	4	1	6	3	8	5

of 10 degrees (**Table 9**). In this context it would be pertinent to make a mention of two adverse points for health. One is the *sixty-fourth navamsha*. This is the navamsha which falls exactly in the eighth house from the natal Moon. In the navamsha chart, it coincides with the fourth house from the location of the Moon. The other is the *twenty-second drekkana*. This is the drekkana that falls exactly in the eighth house from the lagna. In the drekkana chart, it falls in the eighth house. Both these are adverse indicators for health. Lords of sixty-fourth navamsha and twenty-second drekkana, their associates, and grahas located therein are all adverse for health. When dashas adverse for health are in operation, involvement of the sixty-fourth navamsha and twenty-second drekkana add to their virulence. We would leave it to the discretion of the reader about the use of some of the other vargas like the Hora, the Saptamsha, the Dwadashamsha and the Trimshamsha in appropriate situations.

Table 9: The drekkana chart.

	SIGNS											
Drekkana	1	2	3	4	5	6	7	8	9	10	11	12
1st 0° - 10°	1	2	3	4	5	6	7	8	9	10	11	12
2nd 10°-20°	5	6	7	8	9	10	11	12	1	2	3	4
3rd 20°-30°	9	10	11	12	1	2	3	4	5	6	7	8

पश्यन्ति सप्तमं सर्वे शनिजीवकुजाः पुनः ।
विशेषतश्च त्रिदशत्रिकोणचतुरष्टमान् ॥ 5 ॥

5. All (the seven) grahas aspect their seventh house. Additionally, Saturn, Jupiter and Mars have their special aspects on three-ten, five-nine and four-eight houses (respectively).

Comments: Grahas transmit their influence to other houses of the chart and to the grahas located in those houses through their aspects. All grahas aspect their seventh house. They thus also aspect other grahas located in the seventh house from their own position. Besides the seventh house aspect, the outer planets, i.e., Saturn, Jupiter and Mars, have their special aspects. Saturn aspects the third and the tenth houses from its own location, in addition to the seventh house. Jupiter aspects the fifth and the ninth houses in addition to the seventh. And Mars aspects, in addition to the seventh, the fourth and the eighth houses.

About the special aspects, it is felt that these grahas have special functions to perform and they must keep an eye on those special houses aspected by them. The third house is that of courage and the tenth of office and government. Saturn as the natural servant and subordinate often has to take courageous action to carry out the official orders and dictates. It is eminently suited to keep a watch on the third and the tenth houses. The fifth house deals with learning and the ninth with Dharma and moral and spiritual values. Jupiter as the natural Guru keeps an eye on these two houses. The fourth is the house for domestic peace and the eighth for longevity as well as outer aggression. Mars as the army chief must naturally keep a watch on the fourth and the eighth houses.

The above mentioned aspects are the full aspects. Sage Parashara in his classic, the *Brihat Parashara Hora shastra*, however, attributes partial aspects to those grahas which do not have special aspects. These partial aspects are: a quarter aspect on houses 3 and 10, two-quarters (or one half) aspect on houses 5 and 9, and three-quarters aspect on houses 4 and 8. The *Laghu Parashari* only recognizes the complete aspects. Complete aspects alone are thus important here. Partial aspects do not make a yoga fruitful.

CHAPTER 2

फलनिर्णयाध्यायः

Adjudication on Results

सर्वे त्रिकोणनेतारो ग्रहाः शुभफलप्रदाः ।
पतयस्त्रिषडायानां यदि पापफलप्रदाः ॥ 6 ॥

6. All grahas that own trikonas (houses five and nine) behave as benefics. They behave as malefics if they happen to own houses three, six and eleven.

Comments: We have already made a mention of the natural benefics and natural malefics above. From here on, we come to the concept of functional benefics and malefics. Grahas eventually give results according to their functional nature. The natural malefics may behave as benefics and the natural benefics may behave as malefics depending on the lordship of houses in the horoscope. The lordship obviously varies with the different rashis falling in different houses, which ultimately depends upon the rashi falling in the lagna. The grahas thus are subservient to the lagna. As the lagna rashi changes, the rashis falling in different houses, and, therefore, their lords, change.

By trikonas here are meant the houses five and nine. Lords of these houses, i.e., the lords of the rashis falling in these two houses in the horoscope, are considered ever benefic. Thus, even the natural malefics like Mars and Saturn turn benefics when they happen to own either the fifth or the ninth house. Some people like to include the lagna also among the trikonas here. It is better to leave the lagna out of this group for the time being and consider it as a separate entity. The lagna has a special place among the houses of the horoscope. It is considered both a trikona as well as a kendra and has a special benevolence attributed to it.

Planets that own houses three, six and eleven behave as malefics. Thus the best benefic Jupiter also behaves as a malefic if it owns these houses. When natural malefics own these houses, they become worse malefics.

It is important to keep in mind that other than the Sun and the Moon, the remaining five grahas own two rashis each. They could thus own a trikona and an additional house which could be one of those considered malefic by Parashara. It will be noted here, however, that any graha that owns a trikona cannot simultaneously own either the third or the eleventh house. That leaves us with the sixth house. Only Jupiter for Karka lagna and Mercury for Makara lagna each simultaneously own the ninth (a trikona or a benefic) house as well as the sixth (a malefic) house, while Saturn for Kanya lagna simultaneously owns the fifth (a trikona or a benefic) house as well as the sixth (an adverse) house. In these situations, the purely auspicious effects of the trikona lordship would get adulterated.

न दिशन्ति शुभं नृणां सौम्याः केन्द्राधिपा यदि।
क्रूराश्चेदशुभं ह्येते प्रबलाश्चोत्तरोत्तरम्॥ 7 ॥

7. Natural benefics, when they own the kendras, do not indicate benefic results, nor do malefics indicate malefic results when they own the

kendras. These (houses in each of the three groups mentioned above) are progressively stronger.

Comments: The term used for natural benefics in this shloka is 'Saumya', meaning gentle, benevolent and auspicious; for natural malefics the term used is 'Krura', meaning cruel, harsh and destructive. When natural benefics own the kendras, they lose their beneficence. Similarly, the natural malefics shed their maleficence when they own the kendras. Kendras thus have a neutralizing influence. It is again advisable here to consider houses 4, 7 and 10 as the kendras and leave out the lagna which, as already pointed out, has a special benevolent status and whose lord is considered ever benefic. It is also important to point out that mere lordship of a kendra does not convert a benefic into a malefic or a malefic into a benefic. Additional qualifications are required for that change to happen. Thus, for a natural malefic as a kendra lord, it should own another auspicious house to become an outright functional benefic. For example, Saturn as the lord of the tenth house remains a malefic for Mesha lagna where the second house it owns is the adverse eleventh house; not so for Vrisha lagna where it owns the tenth house along with the ninth.

Three groups of houses have been mentioned until now. The trikonas which are auspicious, the three-six-eleven (tri-shad-aaya) group which is inauspicious, and the kendras which are neutralizing in effect. The strength of these groups of houses is as follows: of the trikonas, the ninth house is stronger than the fifth; of the three-six-eleven group, the sixth house is stronger than the third and the eleventh stronger than the sixth; amongst the kendras, the seventh house is stronger than the fourth while the tenth is stronger than the seventh.

Thus, the ninth is the strongest trikona, the tenth the strongest kendra and the eleventh the strongest among the adverse houses.

लग्नाद् व्ययद्वितीयेशौ परेषां साहचर्यतः ।
स्थानान्तरानुगुण्येन भवतः फलदायकौ ॥ 8 ॥

8. Lords of the twelfth and the second houses from the lagna yield results based on their association or according to the other house owned by them.

Comments: The twelfth and the second lords are absolutely neutral, whether by their inherent nature they are benefic or malefic. The way they behave depends on their association or on the other house they own. It is understandable that accumulation of wealth (second house) or its utilization (twelfth house) is neither good nor bad. It all depends on the circumstances, the intent and the means of accumulation or expenditure of wealth. Since the Sun and the Moon only own one rashi each, their lordship of the twelfth house would yield results according to their placement or association. For other grahas which own two houses each, the results depend not only on their placement and association but also on the other house owned by them. These house lords would thus behave as auspicious if the other house owned by them is a trikona, and as inauspicious if the other house owned by them is either of the third or the eleventh.

According to the above principles, Mercury will be beneficial for Vrisha and Tula lagnas as it will simultaneously own a trikona and one of the 2/12 houses. Similarly Jupiter will behave as benefic for Mesha and Vrishchika lagnas because of simultaneously owning a trikona and one of the 2/12 houses. Again, Venus for Mithuna and Kanya lagnas, and Mars for Dhanu and Meena lagnas would behave as benefics by owning one auspicious and one neutral house each.

भाग्यव्ययाधिपत्येन रन्ध्रेशो न शुभप्रदः ।
स एव शुभसन्धाता लग्नाधीशोऽपि चेत्स्वयम् ॥ 9 ॥

9. Being the lord of the twelfth (loss) from the ninth (Bhagya), the eighth lord is not auspicious. It, however, is inclined to become a benefic if it also owns the lagna.

Comments: We have indicated above that the twelfth house from lagna is the house of loss. The twelfth house considered from any other house means loss for that house. The ninth house is the most auspicious house of the horoscope. It indicates, besides several other auspicious aspects, a native's Bhagya or the good fortune ordained by the Lord Almighty based on the individual's past good deeds. The eighth house from the lagna is the twelfth house considered from the ninth house, signifying the loss of whatever the ninth house stands for. Loss of Bhagya is considered as the greatest loss. The eighth house thus qualifies to be the most adverse house of the horoscope.

While stressing upon the maleficence of the eighth house, and consequently of the eighth lord, the author here also highlights the significance of the lagna lord. The maleficence of the eighth lord can be only neutralized and improved upon by its simultaneous lordship of the lagna. This privilege is only available to Mars as the lord of the Mesha lagna and Venus as lord of the Tula lagna because in either case the eighth lord would also happen to be the lagna lord. The question arises that, if the lordship of lagna can erase the blemish of eighth lordship, can it also erase the blemish of the sixth lordship? Mars for Vrishchika lagna and Venus for Vrisha lagna would simultaneously own the lagna and the sixth house. Sage Parashara holds Venus as neutral for Tula lagna and as a malefic for Vrisha lagna. The sage attributes some good effects to Mars for Mesha lagna but only considers it neutral for Vrishchika lagna. This means that even the lagna lordship may not fully erase the blemish of the eighth or sixth lordship in all cases.

Here we come to the categories which the author of the *Laghu Parashari* confers on the different houses:

Trikonas: Houses 5 and 9; ever benefic.

Kendras: Houses 4, 7 and 10; neutralizing.

Tri-shad-aaya: Houses 3, 6 and 11; always adverse.

Vyaya-dwiteeyau: Houses 12 and 2; neutral.

Randhra: Literally, a pit or a crevice; 8th house; most adverse.

Lagna: The ascendant; ever benefic and benevolent.

In the *Brihat Parashara Hora Shaastra*, sage Parashara indicates that the blemish of eighth lordship (as well as the sixth lordship) is wiped off not only by the simultaneous lordship of the lagna but also of a trikona. Thus Jupiter for Simha and Karka lagnas and Mercury for Makara and Kumbha lagnas acquire benefic potential. This privilege does not seem to be granted to Saturn for Mithuna and Kanya lagnas. Another important point to remember is that the blemish of eighth lordship, and its consequent maleficence, is enhanced if the eighth lord simultaneously owns the third house (Mars for Kanya lagna, Venus for Meena lagna) or the seventh house (Saturn for Karka lagna) or the eleventh house (Mercury for Vrishchika lagna, Jupiter for Vrisha lagna).

केन्द्राधिपत्यदोषस्तु बलवान् गुरुशुक्रयोः ।
मारकत्वेऽपि च तयोर्मारकस्थानसंस्थितिः ॥ 10 ॥

बुधस्तदनु चन्द्रोऽपि भवेत्तदनु तद्विधः ।
न रन्ध्रेशत्वदोषस्तु सूर्याचन्द्रमसोर्भवेत् ॥ 11 ॥

10. The blemish of kendra lordship is more intense for Jupiter and Venus; their 'marakatva' (the propensity to 'kill', or make ill) also intensifies if they associate with a maraka house.

11. After these (Jupiter and Venus) comes Mercury (as blemished because of kendra lordship), followed by the Moon. The Sun and the Moon do not suffer blemish of the eighth house lordship.

Comments: It has been already stated that natural benefics get deprived of their beneficence if they happen to own the kendras. Since Jupiter is the best benefic followed by Venus in benevolence, these two suffer the maximum damage to their benefic potential because of kendra lordship. When a rashi owned by Jupiter falls in one kendra, its other rashi too falls in another kendra. In case of Venus, when its one rashi falls in a kendra, the other falls elsewhere. It may be again noted that kendras here mean houses 4, 7 and 10. If Jupiter owns the lagna (in case of Dhanu or Meena lagna), the blemish is not there. If Venus happens to be a yogakaraka (lord of a kendra as well as a trikona, as in case of Makara and Kumbha lagnas), it also loses its malefic potential of kendra lordship. However, if either of these two owns a maraka house, then there does exist a malefic potential. Maraka means 'a killer'. A maraka house and its lord have the potential to either kill the native or disturb his health. The seventh and the second houses are the maraka houses. So if Jupiter or Venus owns the seventh house, there is the blemish of kendra lordship by a natural benefic as well as that of the ownership of a maraka house. This situation of double blemish enhances their maraka potential. In addition, if they are also located in a maraka house, the maraka potential is further enhanced.

For Jupiter, owning the seventh house means that it additionally owns the fourth or the tenth house. Thus this best benefic owns two kendras and behaves as a maraka. When Venus owns the seventh, it additionally owns the second or the twelfth house. The second house is another maraka house. Thus Venus becomes a potent maraka for Mesha lagna, owning two maraka houses, in addition to having the blemish of the kendra lordship. The twelfth house lordship (for Vrishchika lagna) at best is neutral; so Venus would retain its malefic potential of kendra lordship as well as a maraka house lordship. It is emphasized here by the author that the location of either of them in a maraka house further aggravates their maraka potential.

Here arises another point. When Jupiter or Venus owns the seventh house, their placement in the seventh would mean the seventh lord in the seventh house. The seventh lord in the seventh, according to standard teaching of astrology, protects the seventh house. Besides, the placement of a kendra lord in its own house gives rise to one of the powerful Pancha-Mahapurusha yogas. While all this is true, the maraka potential of the maraka grahas persists. Thus the native would enjoy the raja yoga as well as the maraka effect of the grahas concerned. A maraka located in a maraka house does not reduce its malefic potential but only enhances it.

Mercury comes next in order. The rules that apply to Jupiter apply to Mercury as well. For, Mercury too will own two kendras simultaneously and may not suffer much blemish when it owns the lagna. The Moon is the weakest natural benefic and its maraka potential too is not very prominent.

Sage Parashara further holds that the blemish of eighth lordship does not apply to the Sun and the Moon. The Sun would own the eighth house for Makara lagna and the Moon for Dhanu lagna. It may, however, be noted that the eighth lordship of the Sun or the Moon does not completely wipe off their malefic potential. We have particularly noted this in matters of health and disease. **Table 10** shows the benefics, malefics, marakas and yogakarakas for the different lagnas based on the standard Parashari principles.

Table 10: Benefics, malefics, marakas and yoga karakas for different lagnas

<table>
<tr><th></th><th>Lagna</th><th>Benefics</th><th>Malefics</th><th>Marakas</th><th>Yogakaraka</th></tr>
<tr><td>1.</td><td>Mesha</td><td>Sun, Jup</td><td>Mer, Ven, Sat</td><td>Ven</td><td>-</td></tr>
<tr><td></td><td colspan="5">(i) Mere conjunction of Jupiter and Saturn (9th and 10th lords) does not produce a Raja Yoga.
(ii) Jupiter becomes malevolent if ill-associated.
(iii) Mars tends to behave as a benefic on account of the lagna lordship.</td></tr>
<tr><td>2.</td><td>Vrisha</td><td>Sun, Sat</td><td>Mon, Jup Ven</td><td>Mars (Mon, Jup, Ven)</td><td>Sat</td></tr>
<tr><td></td><td colspan="5">(i) Mercury is partly beneficial.
(ii) Even Venus is not too good for Taurus ascendant.</td></tr>
<tr><td>3.</td><td>Mithuna</td><td>Ven</td><td>Sun, Mars Jup</td><td>Mon</td><td>-</td></tr>
<tr><td></td><td colspan="5">(i) Combination of Saturn (9th lord) and Jupiter (7th and 10th lord) does not produce a Rajayoga.
(ii) Jupiter as benefic is the lord of two quadrants (excluding the lagna). It is particularly liable to the blemish of kendra lordship.
(iii) Mercury is neutral. Saturn may give mixed results.</td></tr>
</table>

<table>
<tr><th></th><th>Lagna</th><th>Benefics</th><th>Malefics</th><th>Marakas</th><th>Yogakaraka</th></tr>
<tr><td>4.</td><td>Karka</td><td>Mon, Mars Jup</td><td>Mer, Ven</td><td>Sat</td><td>Mars</td></tr>
<tr><td></td><td colspan="5">(i) Sun acts as a benefic or malefic depending upon its association.</td></tr>
<tr><td>5.</td><td>Simha</td><td>Sun, Mars Jup</td><td>Mer, Ven</td><td>Sat</td><td>Mars</td></tr>
<tr><td></td><td colspan="5">(i) Combination of Jupiter (5th lord) and Venus (10th lord) does not produce a Rajayoga.
(ii) The Moon (12th lord) gives results depending upon its assocation.</td></tr>
<tr><td>6.</td><td>Kanya</td><td>Mer, Ven</td><td>Mon, Mars Jup</td><td>Ven</td><td>-</td></tr>
<tr><td></td><td colspan="5">(i) Association of Venus (9th lord) and Mercury (10th lord and Lagna lord) produces a Rajayoga.
(ii) The Sun (12th lord) gives results based on its association.
(iii) Mercury as lagna lord and 10th lord (the most powerful quadrant) becomes a benefic while Jupiter (4th and 7th lord) suffers from the blemish of lordship of two kendras.</td></tr>
<tr><td>7.</td><td>Tula</td><td>Mer, Sat</td><td>Sun, Mar Jup</td><td>Mars</td><td>Sat</td></tr>
<tr><td></td><td colspan="5">(i) Venus is neutral
(ii) Combination of the Moon (10th lord) with Mercury (9th lord) produces a Rajayoga.</td></tr>
<tr><td>8.</td><td>Vrishchika</td><td>Mon, Jup</td><td>Mer, Ven Sat</td><td>Ven</td><td>-</td></tr>
<tr><td></td><td colspan="5">(i) Mars is neutral (cf. Venus for Taurus lagna).
(ii) The Sun-Moon (10th lord and 9th lord respectively) association produces a Rajayoga.</td></tr>
<tr><td>9.</td><td>Dhanu</td><td>Sun, Mar</td><td>Ven</td><td>Ven, Sat</td><td>-</td></tr>
<tr><td></td><td colspan="5">(i) Jupiter is neutral as is the Moon
(ii) Sun-Mercury (9th and 10th lords) association produces a Rajayoga.</td></tr>
</table>

<table>
<tr><th>Lagna</th><th>Benefics</th><th>Malefics</th><th>Marakas</th><th>Yogakaraka</th></tr>
<tr><td>10. Makara</td><td>Mer, Ven</td><td>Mon, Mar
Jup</td><td>Mar, other
malefics</td><td>Ven</td></tr>
<tr><td colspan="5">(i) The Sun is neutral.
(ii) Saturn (2nd lord) itself is not a maraka as it is the lord of the lagna also.</td></tr>
<tr><td>11. Kumbha</td><td>Ven, Sat</td><td>Mon, Mar
Jup</td><td>Sun, Mar
Jup</td><td>Ven</td></tr>
<tr><td colspan="5">(i) Mercury is mediocre, perhaps more beneficial than harmful.</td></tr>
<tr><td>12. Meena</td><td>Mon, Mar
Jup</td><td>Sun, Mer
Ven, Sat</td><td>Mer, Sat</td><td>-</td></tr>
<tr><td colspan="5">(i) Mars is not a maraka despite being the second lord. (cf. Venus for Virgo ascendant)
(ii) Association of Mars (9th lord) and Jupiter (10th lord as well as lagna lord) produces a Rajayoga.
(iii) Compare this with the role of Jupiter and Mercury in the case of Virgo ascendant</td></tr>
</table>

कुजस्य कर्मनेतृत्वप्रयुक्ता शुभकारिता ।
त्रिकोणस्यापि नेतृत्वे न कर्मेशत्वमात्रतः ॥ 12 ॥

12. The benevolence attributable to Mars as lord of the tenth house (for Karka lagna) is there because it is also the lord of a trikona, and not alone because of the tenth house lordship.

Comments: As already pointed out, the malefics as lords of the kendras lose their maleficence. The tenth house is the strongest of the kendras. A malefic like Mars, when it owns the strongest kendra, only loses its maleficence. The fact of mere tenth house lordship does not automatically convert it into a functional benefic. To attain beneficence, it must additionally own a trikona. That can happen for Karka lagna where Mars owns the tenth house as well as the fifth house (a trikona). This principle is applicable to any malefic. That is, here we should consider Mars as any malefic and also the tenth house as any kendra. The word 'Kuja' used in this shloka, which normally means 'Mars', has been translated by commentators as the one that is '*kutsita*', (कुत्सित) i.e., vile or contemptible, in other words, any natural malefic.

Mars as the lord of a kendra and trikona for Karka lagna behaves as a benefic. For Simha lagna too, it owns a kendra (fourth house) and a trikona (ninth house), hence a benefic. Similarly, Saturn, another malefic owns the fourth and the fifth houses for Tula lagna, and the ninth and the tenth houses for Vrisha lagna; in either case, it behaves as a benefic. It also leads us to the conclusion that a malefic which owns a kendra would behave as an outright functional malefic if it additionally owns any of the adverse houses (houses 3, 6, 8 or 11).

यद्यद्भावगतौ वाऽपि यद्यद्भावेशसंयुतौ ।
तत्तत्फलानि प्रबलौ प्रदिशेतां तमोग्रहौ ॥ 13 ॥

13. The two strong shadow grahas yield results according to whichever houses they occupy and to whichever house lord(s) they associate with.

Comments: The two strong shadow grahas are Rahu and Ketu, the grahas which do not have a physical body. They are mathematical points on the zodiac and (almost) always move in a retrograde direction. They are strong enough to engulf the Sun and the Moon and eclipse them both from time to time. Generally classed as natural malefics, they do not have any effect of their own. However, they produce results in one of the two ways:

1. They behave as the owner of the house they occupy. Thus they are benefic in trikonas, malefic the trishadaaya (3, 6 and 11 houses), neutral (or even benefic to some extent) in kendras, neutral in houses 2 or 12, and very bad in house eight. These are the results they give when located alone in a house.
2. In addition, they give results according to their association:
   (a) Associated with kendra or trikona lords: Good results.
   (b) Associated with the second or the seventh lord: Marakas.
   (c) Associated with the trishadaaya lords or with the eighth lord: Adverse results.
   (d) In the rashis of Mercury and Jupiter: Generally good results.

CHAPTER 3

योगफलाध्यायः

Chapter on Raja Yogas

केन्द्रत्रिकोणपतयः सम्बन्धेन परस्परम् ।
इतरैरप्रसक्ताश्चेद् विशेषफलदायकाः ॥ 14 ॥

14. Lords of kendras and trikonas, when mutually related, and unassociated with others, yield special benefic results.

Comments: We have until now dealt with various aspects of the lordship of grahas. It is time now to analyse the effects of various specific mutual dispositions of grahas which are termed 'yogas' in astrological jargon. When grahas get related to each other in a specific manner, they produce a yoga which yields specific results. Special benefic results are produced when the lords of trikonas and kendras get into some sort of a mutual relationship without any extraneous (non-kendra, non-trikona) interference. Here are the following four ways by which the grahas get mutually related to each other:

1. ***Conjunction:*** When the two grahas are posited together in the same house;
2. ***Mutual aspect:*** When the two grahas mutually aspect each other;
3. ***Exchange:*** Parivartana; the two grahas reside in the rashis of each other;

4. ***Dispositor's aspect:*** That is, aspect by the lord of the rashi in which a graha is posited.

These relationships may be observed in **chart 1** (female native born on April 16, 1944 at 16:36 hours, in Algiers, Algeria). The Sun (lagna lord) and Mercury (second and eleventh lord) are conjoined in the ninth house. The Moon (twelfth lord) and Jupiter (fifth and eighth lord) are in mutual aspect. There is an exchange or Parivartana between the ninth lord Mars and the eleventh lord Mercury. And finally, an exalted Venus, in Jupiter's house, receives the aspect of its dispositor Jupiter. The already mentioned mutual aspect

Venus	Mercury Sun	Saturn	Mars
	Chart 1 (F)		Jupiter Rahu
Moon Ketu	April 16, 1944		Lagna

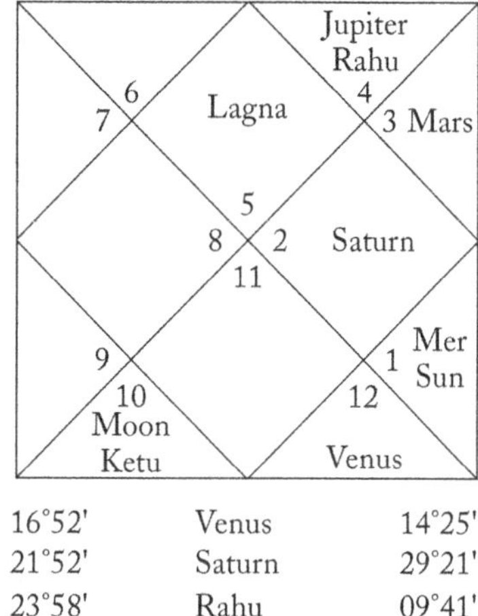

Lagna	17°45'	Mars	16°52'	Venus	14°25'
Sun	03°23'	Mercury	21°52'	Saturn	29°21'
Moon	08°34'	Jupiter	23°58'	Rahu	09°41'

Moon Mars Ketu		Sun	
Jupiter	**Navamsha**		
	Venus	Mercury	Lagna Saturn Rahu

Mercury
8
Venus
7
Lagna
Saturn
Rahu
5
4
6
9
3
12
2
Moon
Mars
Ketu
10
11
Sun
1
Jupiter

between the Moon and Jupiter is further strengthened by the aspect on Jupiter by its dispositor, the Moon.

The *Laghu Parashari* is an elegant text with several terms used here having implied meanings. It gives hints here and there, and the intelligent practitioner of astrology has to arrive at the implied meanings for himself. The text also highlights the beauty of the Sanskrit language which conceals great details in its brevity. The kendras here mean houses 4, 7 and 10 while the trikonas mean houses 5 and 9. The lord of the lagna, which is both a kendra and a trikona, will yield good results whether it associates with another kendra lord or a trikona lord. The lords of these houses by their mutual interrelationship will yield yogas which will produce special benefic results, with the condition that the 'others' do not join these associations. These others must be considered as the lords of the adverse houses like houses 3, 6, 8 and 11. Lords of houses 2 and 12 are neutral and their association does not disturb the quality of the yoga much. Association with the adverse house lords will adulterate the yoga and the 'special' benefic results will be lost to some extent. We would like to tabulate for different lagnas the grahas which own kendras or trikonas, including the lagna, but none of the adverse houses (**see table 11**).

Let us see how a yoga formed by mutual relationship between kendra and trikona lords, when unaffected by others, works. **Chart 2** (male native born on December 1884, at 9:05:30 hours, in Patna, Bihar, India) belongs to Dr Rajendra Prasad, the first President of India. The lagna is Dhanu with the fifth (and twelfth) lord Mars and the tenth (and seventh) lord Mercury located close to each other in the lagna. This yoga caused by the trikona lord Mars and the kendra lord Mercury in Dhanu rashi further receives the aspect of their dispositor, the lagna lord and the best natural benefic Jupiter from the strongest trikona, the ninth house. Thus we have a trikona lord, a kendra lord and the

Table 11: Lagnas and the effectors of yogas.

	Lagna	*Grahas Owning Potentially Yoga-Producing Houses*
1.	Mesha	Sun, Moon, Jupiter, Venus
2.	Vrisha	Sun, Mars, Mercury, Saturn
3.	Mithuna	Mercury, Jupiter, Venus
4.	Karka	Moon, Mars
5.	Simha	Sun, Mars
6.	Kanya	Mercury, Jupiter, Venus
7.	Tula	Moon, Mars, Mercury, Saturn
8.	Vrischika	Sun, Moon, Jupiter, Venus
9.	Dhanu	Sun, Mars, Mercury, Jupiter
10.	Makara	Moon, Venus, Saturn
11.	Kumbha	Sun, Venus, Saturn
12.	Meena	Moon, Mars, Mercury, Jupiter

aspecting lagna lord forming a very potent and benevolent yoga in the lagna. The yoga in the lagna as also the lagna lord that aspects the constituents of the yoga there suffer no blemish of association or aspect of any of the adverse house lords. The native was an educationist, a political

Ketu		Moon Sat (R)	
	Chart 2 (M) December 3, 1884		
			Jupiter
Lagna Mars Mercury	Sun	Venus	Rahu

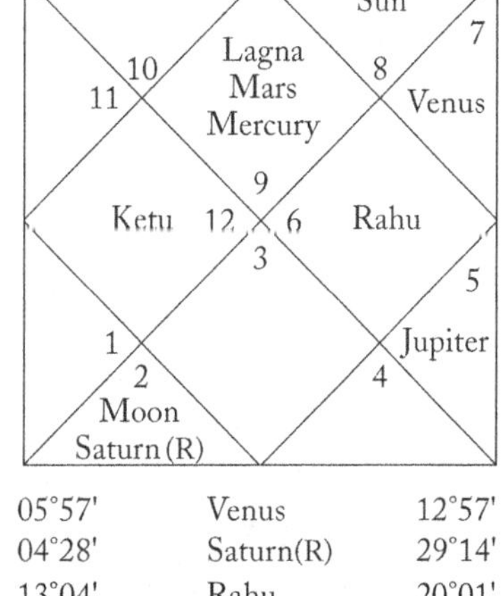

Lagna	23°41'	Mars	05°57'	Venus	12°57'
Sun	19°10'	Mercury	04°28'	Saturn(R)	29°14'
Moon	24°12'	Jupiter	13°04'	Rahu	20°01'

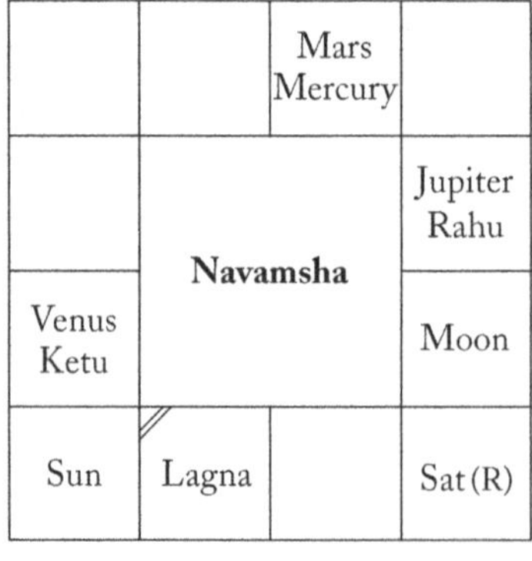

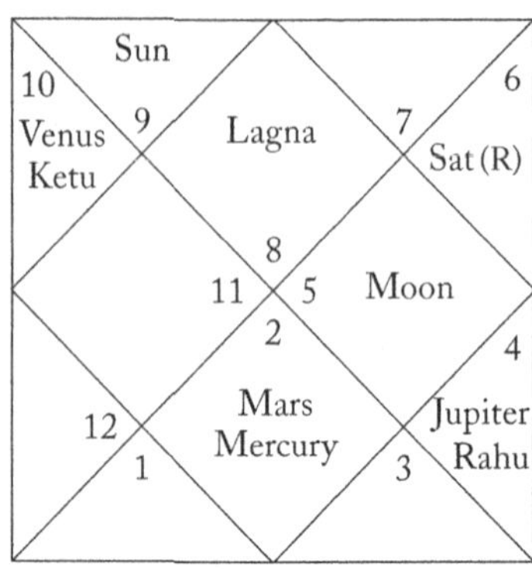

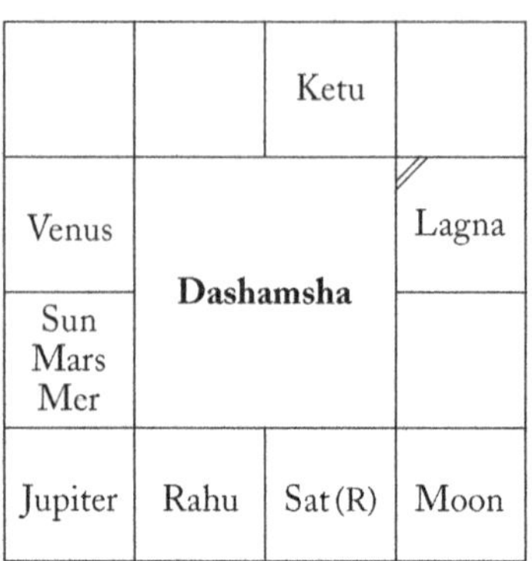

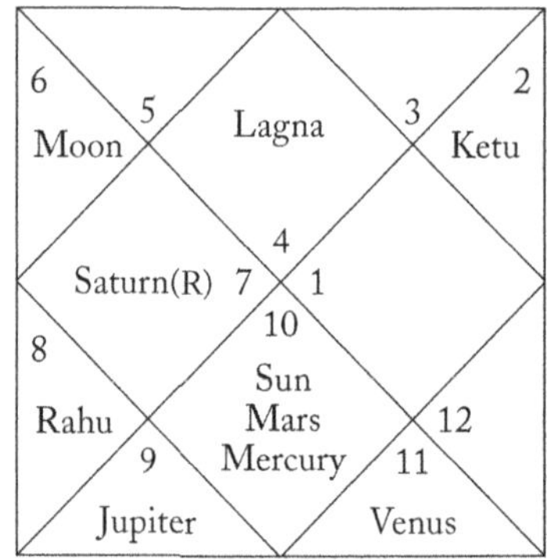

and social activist, and a freedom fighter. Impressed by the dedication, courage and conviction of Mahatma Gandhi, he gave up his lucrative career of a lawyer and came forward to participate in the independence movement. The native in his immense benevolence played a significant role in helping the victims of Bihar and Bengal floods of 1914, the Bihar quake of 1934 and the Quetta quake of 1935. Because of being a part of the Quit India Movement, he remained incarcerated for almost three years (August 8, 1942 to June 15, 1945) (Saturn-Jupiter and Mercury-Mercury periods).

The native was among the most upright, independent, unbiased and highly respected individuals that India has seen during the last century. The dasha of Mercury, the tenth lord, forming an excellent yoga in the lagna, saw him become the President of India on January 26, 1950 (Mercury-Venus dasha) and he remained so till he relinquished office in May 1962 (Ketu-Venus dasha). This sort of a totally unblemished auspicious yoga most certainly promises remarkable results.

The chart under consideration also has another prominent rajayoga, the Gaja-Kesari yoga formed by the mutual kendra disposition of the Moon and Jupiter. The Moon is exalted and Jupiter in the rashi of a natural friend occupies the favourable ninth house. The Moon despite its eighth lordship does not prove adverse as, according to our author, the blemish of eighth house lordship does not apply to the Sun and the Moon. The yoga exists in the dashamsha chart as well.

A Vipareeta rajayoga, or an odd sort of rajayoga, results when the lord of one Trika house occupies another. This yoga would be described in greater details later in this chapter. In the chart under consideration, the eighth lord Moon occupies the sixth house, that too in exaltation. The yoga ensures name and fame for the native. While this yoga is not as potent as a Gaja-Kesari yoga which is already there, it still adds to the fame and renown that the native would have enjoyed otherwise.

Let us have a look at another chart with Dhanu lagna where an important yoga obtains according to the definition given above though with some modification. The native of **chart 3** (male native, born on August 26, 1956, at 15:45 hours IST, in Delhi, India) has his lagna lord Jupiter join the ninth lord Sun in the ninth house forming a potent rajayoga. The lagna lord is supposed to be both a kendra and a trikona lord and qualifies to form a favourable yoga with either another kendra lord or another trikona lord. This yoga in the ninth house is aspected by another trikona lord Mars from the third house. The retrogression of Mars as well as its link with the adverse Saturn through exchange

	Moon	Ketu	Venus
Mars (R)	**Chart 3 (M)** August 26, 1956		
			Sun Jupiter
Lagna	Saturn Rahu		Mercury

11 Mars (R) 10
Lagna
Saturn Rahu 8 7
9
12 6 Mercury
3
1 Moon
Venus
5 Sun Jupiter
2 Ketu
4

Lagna	17°58'	Mars (R)	28°47'	Venus	24°09'
Sun	09°52'	Mercury	06°35'	Saturn	03°28'
Moon	06°07'	Jupiter	16°49'	Rahu	10°05'

	Ketu	Moon Venus	Sun Mars(R)
Mercury	**Navamsha**		
			Saturn
		Rahu	Lagna Jupiter

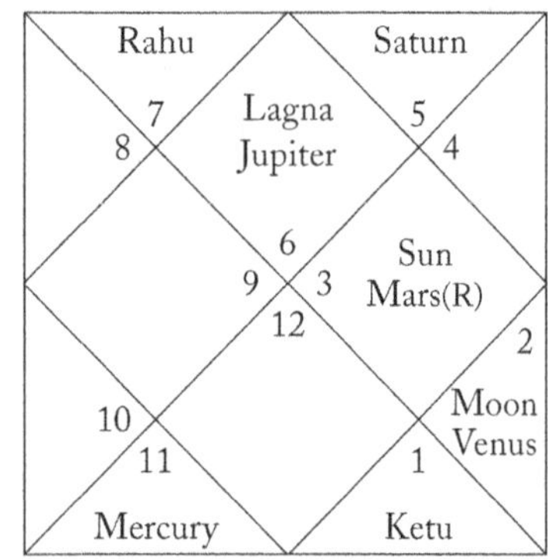

	Ketu	Lagna	Moon
Venus	**Dashamsha**		Mercury
Jupiter			Saturn
	Sun Mars (R)	Rahu	

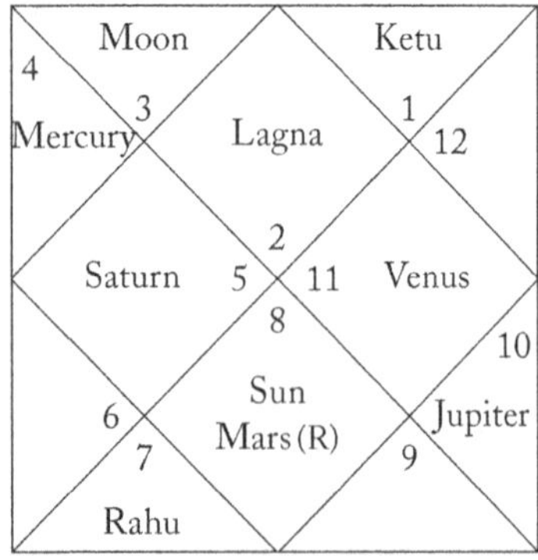

of houses (Parivartana yoga) constitutes a blemish. This yoga also receives the aspect of Saturn from the twelfth house. Saturn is the lord of houses 2 and 3, one a neutral house and the other a malefic house, an additional blemish even though the third is the weakest of the malefic houses. So the yoga does get blemished, limiting to a large extent the great status and fame that the yoga would otherwise confer on the native. In any case this is a strong rajayoga occurring in the ninth house making the native highly fortunate. It goes without saying that only unblemished yogas would give unblemished results. Incidentally, the native has been unusual on another account in that he happened to remember his past life. His was one of the most widely reported cases in India and formed the first chapter of the book *"Cases of the Reincarnation Type: Ten Cases in India"* by Professor Ian Stevenson of the Virginia University in USA.

केन्द्रत्रिकोणनेतारौ दोषयुक्तावपि स्वयम् ।
सम्बन्धमात्राद्बलिनौ भवेतां योगकारकौ ॥ 15 ॥

15. Strong kendra and trikona lords, even when themselves blemished, yield highly benefic (yoga-karaka) results due to their mutual relationship alone.

Comments: The mere association of a kendra lord with a trikona lord yields yoga-karaka results. The term 'yoga-karaka' is used to indicate a graha or a yoga which tends to raise the social, financial as well as official status of the individual. The term is often used interchangeably with 'raja-yoga-karaka' which literally means a high status equivalent to that of a king. When these lords get blemished, they do produce raja yoga but it is not as clean and unadulterated as we have seen in our earlier discussion. The possible blemishes of the kendra and trikona lords could be:

1. Simultaneous lordship of houses 3, 6, 8 or 11 by the kendra lords, or that of houses 6 or 8 by the trikona lords;
2. Association with the lords of houses 3, 6, 8 or 11;
3. Debilitation, combustion, inimical placement, defeat in graha-yuddha, Paapa-Kartari, etc.

Graha-yuddha or planetary warfare is supposed to exist between any two grahas from Mars to Saturn (excluding the Sun and the Moon) when they happen to be conjunct and within one degree longitude of each other. Generally the graha that is farther advanced of the two is considered the loser. Defeat in graha-yuddha is supposed to be a weakness. It may be noted that the conditions mentioned under point '3' above render the graha weak and may actually negate the formation of raja yoga. The stipulation here is that the yoga forms when strong kendra and trikona lords meet. So that basically leaves us with the adverse houses and their lords/lordship to provide blemish. Another meaning that this shloka might convey is that a rajayoga is formed when the lords of the ninth house (the strongest trikona) and the tenth house (the strongest kendra) unite; they would produce good results even when blemished, though it is desirable that they do not own the eighth or the eleventh house simultaneously. We are of the opinion that a relationship between a kendra lord and a trikona lord undoubtedly produces yoga-karaka results. However, these results get tinged by the additional qualifications that the grahas acquire by their so-called blemish.

Let have a look at **chart 4** belonging to the former Indian Prime Minister, Smt. Indira Gandhi (born on November 19, 1917, at 23.11 hours IST, in Allahabad, India). Her chart has the special feature of three Parivartana yogas or

		Jupiter (R)	Ketu
	Chart 4 (F) November 19, 1917		Lagna Saturn
Moon			Mars
Venus Rahu	Sun Mercury		

Mars 5 6 Lagna Saturn Ketu 3 2 Jupiter (R) 4 7 1 10 8 Sun Mer Moon 12 11 9 Venus Rahu

Lagna	27°22'	Mars	16°22'	Venus	21°00'
Sun	04°07'	Mercury	05°35'	Saturn	21°47'
Moon	05°35'	Jupiter (R)	15°00'	Rahu	09°12'

Lagna		Jupiter (R)	Rahu
Moon	**Navamsha**		
Saturn			Sun Mars
Ketu		Mercury Venus	

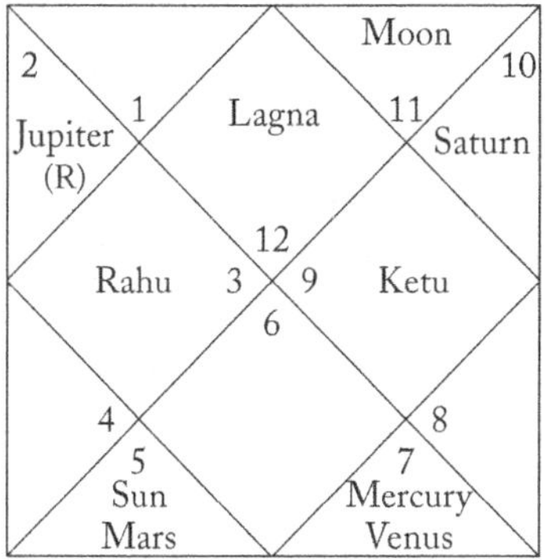

Rahu			Jupiter (R)
	Dashamsha		Venus
Mars			Sun
Lagna	Mercury	Moon Saturn	Ketu

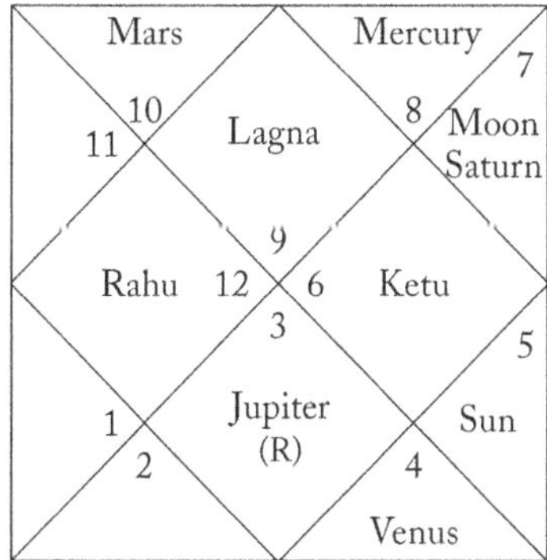

exchanges. There is an exchange between the lagna lord and the seventh lord, between the second lord and the fifth lord, and between the sixth lord and the eleventh lord. The two points that we want to highlight here are:

1. The exchange between the Moon, the lagna lord, and Saturn, the seventh or a kendra lord, is blemished by the eighth house lordship of Saturn.
2. The exchange between Venus, the fourth house or a kendra lord, and Jupiter, the ninth house or a trikona lord, is blemished by eleventh house lordship of Venus and sixth house lordship of Jupiter. In this yoga, even the placement of Venus and Jupiter is in adverse houses.

Despite the blemishes mentioned above, she enjoyed rajayoga both in the dashas of Jupiter and Saturn. Saturn actually made her more powerful and a leader of the masses. She managed to dismember Pakistan in the 1971 war in the Saturn dasha only. Despite several fluctuations in her career, she remained significant right till her end which too came in the Saturn dasha. Saturn is a malefic lord of a kendra, exchanging houses with the lagna lord Moon, but is also the lord of the most adverse eighth house, which by implication is the house of death.

We have discussed above how a mutual relationship between a kendra and trikona lord yields benefic results. This relationship may be in any of the four manners already discussed. In the chart above, the mutual relationship was primarily due to exchanges though in one of the two yogas discussed a mutual aspect was also involved. We have another example (**chart 6**) where there is an association of a yogakaraka Mars (which owns a trikona and a kendra) with the fourth house (a kendra) lord Venus in the ninth house, and which the reader will find interesting. That will be discussed in the comments to Shloka 19.

निवसेतां व्यत्ययेन तावुभौ धर्मकर्मणोः ।
एकत्रान्यतरो वाऽपि वसेच्चेद्योगकारकौ ॥ 16 ॥

16. Lords of the ninth and the tenth houses when located in each other's house, or together in either house, or when either is located in the other's house, tend to yield yoga-karaka results.

Comments: Three different situations leading to yoga-karaka results are presented here:

1. Ninth lord in the tenth house and tenth lord in the ninth house;
2. Ninth and tenth lords together in the ninth or the tenth house;
3. Ninth lord in the tenth house or tenth lord in the ninth house.

It has been already emphasized that the lords of the kendras and the trikonas when mutually related produce raja yogas. In the present shloka, the importance of the kendras and the trikonas, and not just their lords, is stressed upon. Thus when the ninth and the tenth house lords exchange houses, they produce a potent raja-yoga. Another potent raja-yoga results when the ninth and the tenth lords are located together in either the ninth house or the tenth house. What is less often appreciated is that the ninth lord alone in the tenth house, or the tenth lord alone in the ninth house, also produces a raja-yoga. Thus the association of the ninth lord with the tenth house or that of the tenth lord with the ninth house is also important. Of the three categories of yogas indicated here, the first one is the strongest and the last one the weakest.

Here again, it is important to appreciate that the meaning of the ninth house here has to be extended to imply the trikonas and the tenth house the kendras. If we remember that the ninth house is the strongest trikona and tenth the strongest kendra, the yogas their lords would produce would be of the strongest quality. When the ninth house and the tenth house represent respectively the trikonas and kendras, their lords in various possible combinations will give us a variety of different raja-yogas of different potencies. These may be indicated below:

1. Between the fourth lord and the fifth lord:
   (a) 4L in 5H, 5L in 4H;
   (b) 4L and 5L in either 4H or 5H;
   (c) 4L in 5H or 5L in 4H.
2. Between the fourth lord and the ninth lord:
   (a) 4L in 9H and 9L in 4H;
   (b) 4L and 9L in either 4H or 9H;
   (c) 4L in 9H or 9L in 4H.
3. Between the seventh lord and fifth lord:
   (a) 7L in 5H and 5L in 7H;
   (b) 7L and 5L in either 7H or 5H;
   (c) 7L in 5H or 5L in 7H.
4. Between the seventh lord and ninth lord:
   (a) 7L in 9H and 9L in 7H;
   (b) 7L and 9L in either 7H or 9H;
   (c) 7L in 9H or 9L in 7H.
5. Between the tenth lord and the fifth lord:
   (a) 10L in 5H and 5L in 10H;
   (b) 10L and 5L in either 10H or 5H;
   (c) 10L in 5H or 5L in 10H.

6. Between the tenth lord and the ninth lord (already mentioned above):
   (a) 10L in 9H and 9L in 10H;
   (b) 10L and 9L in either 10H or 9H;
   (c) 10L in 9H or 9L in 10H.

One can thus conceive several raja-yogas of varying natures and potentials. As already pointed out, the additional house lordships of these various grahas would tinge the raja-yogas variously to produce varying results.

त्रिकोणाधिपयोर्मध्ये सम्बन्धो येन केनचित्।
केन्द्रनाथस्य बलिनो भवेद्यदि सुयोगकृत्॥ 17॥

17. A good and benefic yoga is produced when a trikona lord establishes any relationship with a strong kendra lord.

Comments: An alternate or an additional meaning of the above shloka is: A good and benefic yoga is produced when a strong trikona lord establishes any relationship with a kendra lord.

There seems to be some repetition of this principle. It has been already stressed upon that any mutual relationship between a kendra lord and a trikona lord is to be considered beneficial. One interpretation of a 'strong kendra lord' is the tenth lord. Similarly, a 'strong trikona lord' is the ninth lord. Thus relationship between any kendra lord with the ninth lord, or of any trikona lord with the tenth lord, should produce a raja-yoga.

As we have mentioned above, this principle has already been stressed upon in the earlier verses. So, is it just a repetition of the earlier principles or does this mean something different? It appears to us that strength here should be considered in terms of not the house lordship but the actual strength of a graha. A graha attains strength when it is in its own house, in its Moolatrikona, in exaltation, or in strength in the navamsha. We shall further elaborate this principle while discussing **chart 6** under the comments to shloka 19.

दशास्वपि भवेद्योगः प्रायशो योगकारिणोः ॥
दशाद्वयीमध्यगतस्तदयुक् शुभकारिणाम् ॥ 18 ॥

18. Dashas of yoga-producing grahas (kendra and trikona lords) often yield favourable results. Between two yoga-karaka dashas, the dashas of benefics unrelated with yoga-karakas also yield good results.

Comments: The results of favourable yogas tend to fructify during the dashas of the grahas that constitute that yoga. Especially important are the mahadasha of a yogakaraka and the antardashas also of yogakarakas. Between the antardashas of two yoga-karaka grahas, if there fall the dashas of other benefics unrelated to them or to the mahadasha lord, those antardashas would still yield favourable results. The importance of a graha related or unrelated to yoga-causing grahas is stressed in this shloka (as well as in the subsequent one). A graha would be favourably affected if it has some relationship with a yoga-forming graha. However, the dasha of a benefic graha which is unrelated to yoga-forming grahas, is still likely to produce favourable results when it falls between two favourable dashas. Obviously, the intervening dasha of this benefic graha would produce far superior results if it were related to the yoga-producing graha(s) in any of the four manners already discussed. The corollary of this principle would be that the dasha of an unrelated benefic falling between two adverse dashas would also prove to be adverse! This looks somewhat like the principle behind the Kartari yogas. A graha hemmed between two malefics is prone to deliver malefic results while one hemmed between two benefic grahas will tend to give benefic results.

योगकारकसम्बन्धात् पापिनोऽपि ग्रहाः स्वतः।
तत्तद्भुक्त्यनुसारेण दिशेयुर्योगजं फलम् ॥ 19 ॥

19. The Paapa-grahas too, because of their relationship with yogakarakas, themselves indicate appropriate yoga results during their antardashas.

Comments: The above two shlokas indicate the nature of results which one may expect during the mahadasha of a yogakaraka and the antardashas of two yogakarakas interposed by an unrelated benefic or a related malefic. Thus, between two yogakaraka dashas (AD's), the dasha (AD) of an unrelated benefic graha would be likely to produce benefic result. In case of the dashas (AD's) of Paapa grahas falling between two yogakaraka dashas (AD's), the good results would be experienced only if the Paapa grahas happen to be related to or connected with the yogakaraka grahas. In case an intervening bad dasha lord does not get related to the yogakaraka dashas surrounding it, or to the yogakaraka mahadasha lord, the good results may not be experienced.

Let us have a look at **chart 5** (female native, born on September 29, 1954 at 14:38 hours IST, at 13°N05', 80°E17', India). With Makara lagna, she has a very strong tenth house with the lagna lord and the tenth lord both located in the tenth house. In addition, there are the seventh lord

			Ketu
	Chart 5 (F) September 29, 1954		Jupiter
Lagna			
Mars Rahu		Moon Mercury Venus Saturn	Sun

Mars Rahu 9 8
11 12 Lagna
10 1 7 4
Moon Mercury Venus Saturn 6
2 Jupiter Sun
3 5
Ketu

Lagna	14°50'	Mars	23°16'	Venus	25°57'
Sun	12°27'	Mercury	07°01'	Saturn	14°35'
Moon	08°23'	Jupiter	03°06'	Rahu	17°13'

Ketu	Sun	Lagna Venus	
Saturn	**Navamsha**		Jupiter
Moon Mercury		Mars	Rahu

Sun
4 12
3 Lagna Venus 1
Jupiter Ketu
2
5 11 Saturn
8
6
Rahu 10
7 9
Mars Moon Mercury

	Jupiter	Rahu	Venus
Saturn	**Dashamsha**		Mars
Lagna			
Moon Mercury	Ketu		Sun

Saturn Moon Mercury 8
11 9
12 Lagna Ketu
10
Jupiter 1 7
4
2 6
Rahu Mars Sun
3 5
Venus

Moon and the ninth lord Mercury. We have in this combination three kendra lords and two trikona lords joining in the tenth house. The exalted lagna lord in the tenth house, the tenth lord in the tenth house and an exalted Jupiter in the seventh house form three potent 'Pancha-Mahapurusha' yogas making this chart extremely strong. The strength of the lagna lord and the tenth lord persists in the navamsha and the dashamsha charts as well. The disposition of the grahas in the chart indicates this to be a powerful chart. Within a short time after having moved to USA, the native achieved a big name in the world of business. Today she is a recognized leader in the worlds of business, education and the arts. She is a renowned philanthropist and a Grammy-nominated musician. She has contributed immensely toward education and health, and has a strong faith in meditation and spirituality.

We shall try to confine ourselves to the matter related with the shlokas above. Her Saturn dasha operated from May 31, 1986 to May 31, 2005. Sage Parashara states that important events happen during the dashas of the lagna lord, the tenth lord and the exalted grahas. Here we have the mahadasha of a yoga-producing graha. As we shall also find out later, the antardasha of a graha during its own mahadasha does not give any significant results. After Saturn-Saturn was over, there came the dasha of Saturn-Mercury (June 3, 1989 to February 11, 1992), during which she founded a financial advisory company, restructuring several prominent financial institutions all over. She created billions of dollars in the process. Mercury, a trikona lord, joins three kendra lords, including the lagna lord, in the tenth house. Saturn-Venus was one of the best times of her life as far her finances and her prominence in the world of business were concerned. Venus, as we see, is the yogakaraka involved in the big raja-yoga in the tenth house. Our concern is the intervening dasha of Saturn-Ketu (February 11, 1992 to March 22, 1993). Ketu is a natural malefic and located in the malefic sixth house, aspected by another malefic Mars. It is supposed to bring to the fore the adverse lordship of Mercury and spoil the rajayoga. However, our classic says that between two yogakaraka dashas, the intervening malefic dasha too yields good results only. The native continued to enjoy the rajayoga effects during Ketu antardasha too.

Before going further with the next example, we would like the reader to recall our comments to shloka 17 above. We have clarified there that a rajayoga would result when a strong kendra lord gets connected with a trikona lord, or a strong trikona lord gets connected with a kendra lord. We have mentioned there that the strength of the kendra lord or the trikona lord should be based on the inherent strength of the graha, like its own house, exaltation, moolatrikona or vargottama.

Chart 6 (male native, born on February 4, 1921 at 17 hours IST, in Cochin, India) belongs to an erstwhile President of India who came from an extremely ordinary background but attained the highest position in the country by sheer perseverance, dedication and hard work. In this chart with Karka lagna, the yogakaraka Mars associates with Venus in the ninth house. Venus is the lord of the fourth house, a kendra, and Mars the lord of the fifth house, a trikona, as also of the strongest kendra, the tenth house. The point here is that Mars the trikona lord joins a kendra lord that is exalted. Thus, the trikona lord Mars forms a rajayoga here with a strong kendra lord Venus. Incidentally, this Venus is debilitated in the navamsha with a cancellation of debilitation. This combination in the auspicious ninth house is aspected by another kendra lord Saturn with the disqualifications of being also the eighth lord and retrograde. The strong and fortunate combination forms in the ninth house though with some deficiency.

Mars Venus	Ketu		
Mercury	**Chart 6 (M)** February 4, 1921		Lagna
Sun			Jupiter (R)
Moon		Rahu	Saturn (R)

Jupiter (R) 6
Saturn (R) 5
Lagna 4
3
2
Rahu 7
1 Ketu
10 Sun
12 Mars Venus
8
9 Moon
11 Mercury

Lagna	02°01'	Mars	00°33'	Venus	09°02'
Sun	22°22'	Mercury	05°37'	Saturn (R)	01°11'
Moon	13°47'	Jupiter (R)	24°36'	Rahu	07°55'

			Ketu
	Navamsha		Lagna Sun Mars
Saturn (R)			Moon
Rahu	Jup(R) Mer		Venus

6 Moon
5 Venus
4 Lagna Sun Mars
3 Ketu
2
7
1
10 Saturn (R)
8 Jup(R) Mer
9 Rahu
12
11

Lagna Mercury	Sun Moon Jup(R)	Saturn (R)	Ketu
Venus	**Dashamsha**		
Rahu	Mars		

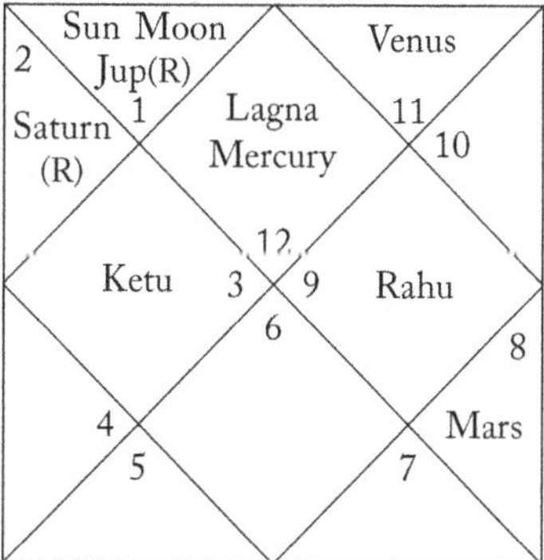

Another yoga may be found here because of the lagna lord Moon in the sixth house aspected by Jupiter. The Moon occupies the sign Dhanu belonging to Jupiter. It is aspected by its dispositor who is not only the adverse sixth lord but also the auspicious ninth lord. Jupiter's aspect on the tenth house or tenth lord in rashi, navamsha and dashamsha indicates benevolence, high ethics and moral values exercised while performing one's duty. Jupiter is particularly significant in the dashamsha because of its association with the two luminaries, one of which is exalted.

The native had some hard time during his early years but persevered and acquired a post-graduate degree in India. After working as a journalist in Delhi for some time, he left for the UK in 1945 where he studied political science. He returned to India in 1948 and met the then Prime Minister Pt. Jawahar Lal Nehru. On Nehru's request, the native joined the Indian Foreign Service as a Diplomat. The date of joining was April 18, 1949. Moon-Rahu (October 30, 1947 to April 29, 1949) was just ending and Moon-Jupiter (April 29, 1949 to August 29, 1950) was about to begin. From years 1967 to 1978, during most of the Rahu dasha, starting from Rahu-Jupiter (with effect from February 9, 1966) and ending sometime with Rahu-Sun (ending on November 10, 1978), he worked as an ambassador to several countries. Rahu in a kendra, with its exalted dispositor forming a potent rajayoga in the ninth house, is eminently suited to involve the native in important government business related to foreign countries. Nehru is supposed to have termed the native, during the latter's early years in the Indian Foreign Service, as "the best diplomat of the country". Between 1980 and 1984, the native served as the Indian Ambassador to the United States during the regime of Indira Gandhi and was instrumental in improving the relations between the two countries. During this period, he moved out of Rahu dasha and moved into Jupiter.

On the advice of the then Prime Minister, Indira Gandhi, the native entered politics. He won three elections to the Lok Sabha, in 1984, 1989 and 1991. During this period the dashas that operated were Jupiter-Saturn (July 18, 1983 to January 28, 1986), Jupiter-Mercury (January 28, 1986 to May 5, 1988), Jupiter-Ketu (May 5, 1988 to April 11, 1989) and Jupiter-Venus (April 11 to December 11, 1991). Jupiter-Saturn is the dasha of a trikona lord and the antardasha of a kendra lord, generally a favourable situation. Jupiter-Mercury means the antardasha of a malefic house lord, located in a malefic house, exchanging houses with the highly malefic eighth lord Saturn. The next antardasha is that of Ketu, the shadowy graha located in a benefic house, the tenth. Its dispositor is located in the favourable ninth house, associated with an exalted kendra lord forming a rajayoga in the ninth house. Ketu itself is aspected by the mahadasha lord and ninth lord Jupiter. This has to be a favourable dasha. The adverse Mercury dasha falling between two benefic dashas also yielded good results only, more so because the antardasha lord Mercury is connected with the mahadasha lord Jupiter through mutual aspect. The next dasha was Jupiter-Venus, another dasha of yoga-forming grahas.

The native next served as the Vice President of India from August 21, 1992 to July 24, 1997, and as President of India from July 25, 1997 to July 25, 2002. This phase started with Jupiter-Sun and ended with Saturn-Mercury (December 11, 1991 to February 9, 2003). We have already discussed about the mahadasha lord Jupiter. The Sun is fairly strong in both the navamsha and the dashamsha, being under a lot of benefic influence. The reader is advised to take note of another strong rajayoga. When both the Sun and the Moon are under the influence of Jupiter in the dashamsha chart, this forms a potent rajayoga ensuring high status and fame. In this case, Jupiter as the lagna lord of the dashamsha chart associates with an exalted Sun and the fifth lord Moon in the second house. Saturn dasha started in May 1997. The dasha at the conclusion of his Presidency was Saturn-Mercury (June 1, 2000 to February 9, 2003). We have already discussed the maleficence of Mercury. The political ambience of the time did not give him a chance for a second term of Presidency. A malefic mahadasha (of Saturn) during a malefic antardasha (of Mercury), with the AD lord related to the MD lord by Parivartana yoga, did not permit any continuation of the rajayoga. The principle is thus clear. The dasha of malefic AD lord related to a benefic MD lord and intervening between two benefic dashas is likely to prove beneficial; the dasha of a malefic AD lord related to a malefic MD lord is likely to produce adverse results. The reader is referred to comments to shlokas 37 and 38 for further clarification.

The native did a lot of work concerning social and economic justice. He was an educationist and a reformist. After demitting office, he continued with social work. He finally left this world on November 9, 2005 in the dasha of Saturn-Venus (March 20, 2004 to May 21, 2007). Saturn is a maraka, being the lord of the seventh (and the eighth) house(s). Retrograde, and aspected by a natural malefic Mars, it supersedes others in maraka potential as we shall learn later. The antardasha lord Venus, being the malefic lord of the eleventh house and under the influence of a strong maraka Saturn precipitates the event. These principles are mentioned later in the text. Another principle mentioned later states that during the dasha of Saturn-Venus, the latter would give the results of Saturn instead of its own. Hence, Venus gives the results of the maraka mahadasha lord Saturn.

केन्द्रत्रिकोणाधिपयोरेकत्वे योगकारकौ।
अन्यत्रिकोणपतिना सम्बन्धो यदि किं परम् ॥ 20 ॥

20. When the same graha owns a kendra and a trikona, it becomes a yoga-karaka. What could be better if it also gets related with another trikona lord?

Comments: We have realized by now that a mutual relationship between a kendra and a trikona lord produces a raja-yoga. When the same graha owns both a kendra and a trikona, that graha attains special propensity to do good. The term used for such a graha is 'yoga-karaka'. Not all grahas can own both a kendra and a trikona in the same chart, and not all lagna charts have such yoga-karakas. This right is granted only to three grahas and six lagnas. For the lagnas of the Sun and the Moon (Simha and Karka lagnas), Mars happens to be the yogakaraka, being in either case the lord of a trikona and a kendra. For the lagnas of Venus (Vrisha and Tula), Saturn happens to be the yogakaraka. For the lagnas of Saturn (Makara and Kumbha), Venus happens to be the yogakaraka. A yogakaraka is considered to be a highly beneficial graha. The author here intends to imply that a highly benefic graha, a yoga-karaka, would produce far superior results if it were to additionally associate with another trikona lord.

Chart 7 (female native, born on June 4, 1975 at 09:09 hours, in Los Angeles, California, USA) belongs to a celebrated American actress who is also a filmmaker and a strong advocate of rights of women, refugees and children. Karka lagna rises with the natural benefic Venus very close to the degree of the lagna. The proximity of Venus, the beautiful and artistic graha, to the lagna belonging to another beautiful graha, the Moon, confers on her all beauty

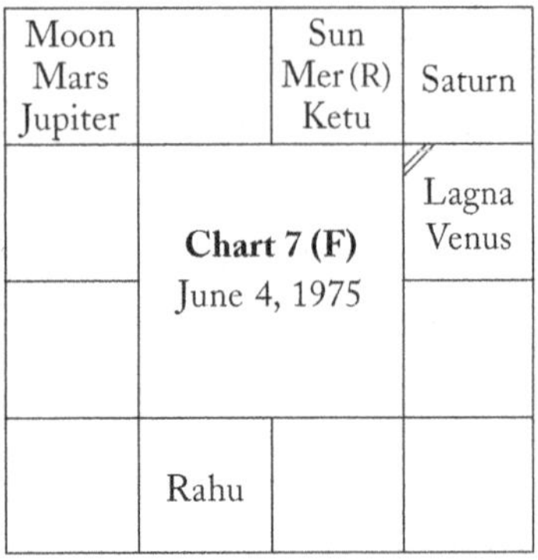

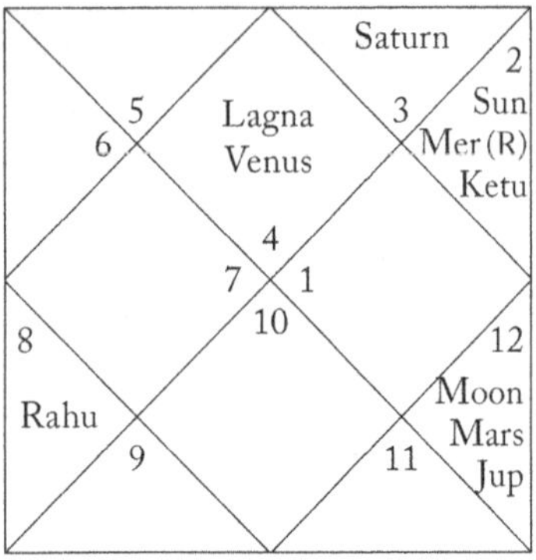

Moon Mars Jupiter		Sun Mer (R) Ketu	Saturn
	Chart 7 (F) June 4, 1975		Lagna Venus
	Rahu		

Lagna Venus 4
Saturn 3
2 Sun Mer (R) Ketu
1
12 Moon Mars Jup
11
10
Rahu 9
8
7
6
5

Lagna	05°22'	Mars	17°11'	Venus	04°38'
Sun	19°54'	Mercury (R)	28°48'	Saturn	23°52'
Moon	19°34'	Jupiter	23°54'	Rahu	07°22'

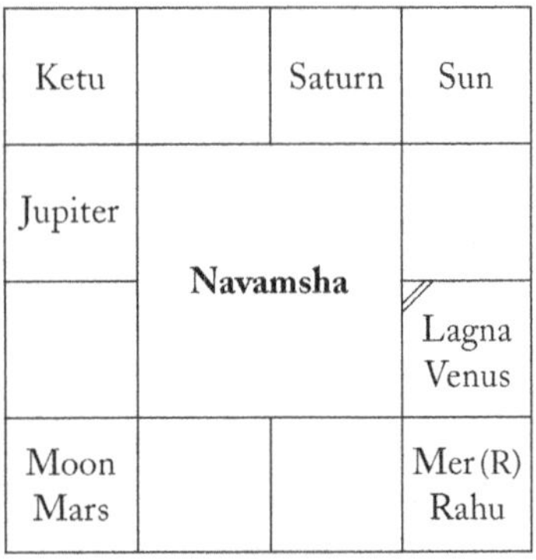

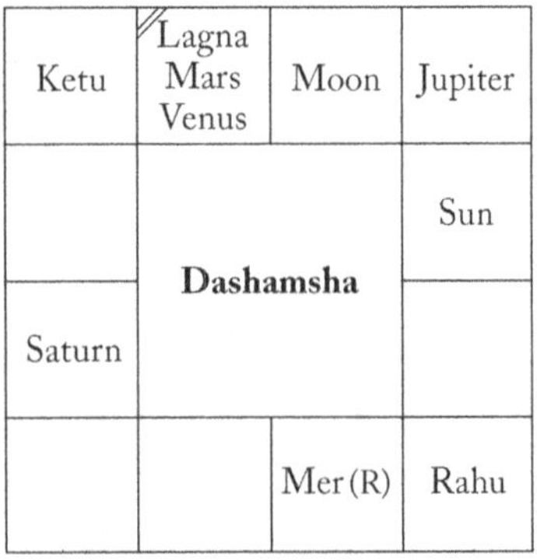

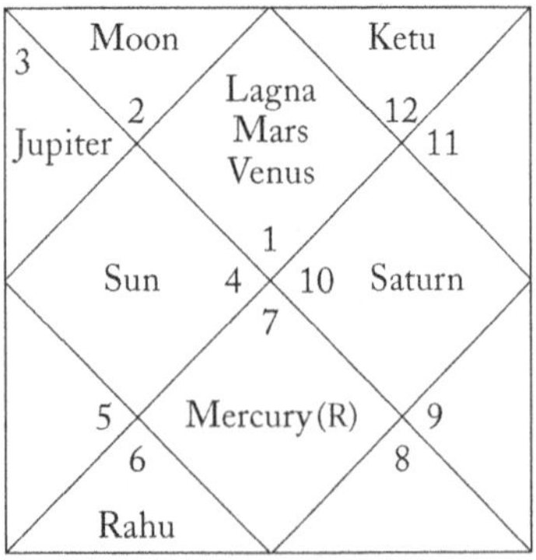

Ketu		Saturn	Sun
Jupiter	**Navamsha**		
			Lagna Venus
Moon Mars			Mer (R) Rahu

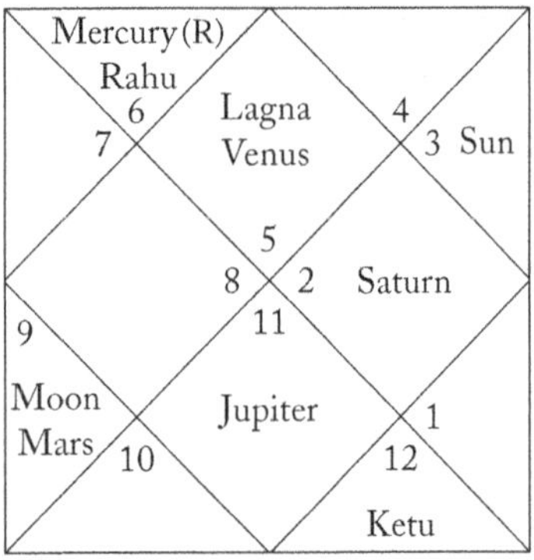

Lagna Venus 5
4
3 Sun
Saturn 2
1
Ketu 12
Jupiter 11
Moon Mars 10
9
8
7
Mercury (R) Rahu 6

Ketu	Lagna Mars Venus	Moon	Jupiter
	Dashamsha		Sun
Saturn			
		Mer (R)	Rahu

Lagna Mars Venus 1
Ketu 12
11
Saturn 10
9
8
Mercury (R) 7
Rahu 6
5
Sun 4
3
Moon Jupiter 2

and rare creativity. This Venus, because of its proximity to the degree of the lagna, remains in the lagna in several of the varga charts, emphasizing its impact on the persona of the native. No wonder she was cited as the world's most beautiful woman by several media outlets for several years.

For Karka lagna, Mars is a highly benefic graha, a yogakaraka, as already pointed out in an earlier verse. This yogakaraka is located in the strongest trikona, the ninth house, in association with the ninth lord Jupiter. This makes it a highly beneficial yoga in the ninth house. Another factor adds benevolence to this yoga: The lagna lord Moon also joins this combination, being very close to the yogakaraka Mars. Thus we have all trikona lords (including the lagna lord) in the ninth house, of which Mars is also a kendra lord. What an extremely benevolent yoga in the ninth house in addition to a highly benevolent disposition of the lagna!

The native has been an extremely successful, highly awarded, American actress. She has been cited as one of the most influential and powerful people in America's entertainment industry. She has earned renown for her humanitarian work all over the globe where she promotes various causes. Some of the important issues that she concerns herself with include women's rights, child education, immigration, and issues pertaining to refugees. For her pioneering work for the welfare of refugees, she has been appointed a Special Envoy for the United Nations High Commissioner for Refugees (UNHCR). Despite her several personal issues, with the malefic Saturn aspecting this highly benevolent yoga in the ninth house and itself being aspected by Mars, the benevolence of this benefic yoga cannot be ignored. The same beauty and benevolence are obvious in the navamsha and dashamsha charts too. Especially obvious in the navamsha are the two first rate benefics in the lagna/seven axis, and the lagna lord in the eleventh house aspected by the two trikona lords Mars and Jupiter, as also by the Moon.

It may be of some interest to compare the above chart with another one (**Chart 8:** Marilyn Monroe, born on June 1, 1926, at 9:30 hours, at Los Angeles, California, USA) with a similar yoga and see how different dispositions of a similar yoga produce different results. She too was an American actress and one of the most popular sex symbols of the 1950's and early 1960's.

Here too, the lagna is Karka and Mars happens to be the yoga-karaka, being the lord of the tenth house and the fifth house. Here too, the yoga-karaka unites with the ninth lord Jupiter, a highly benefic combination, conferring fame and prominence on the native. However, this raja-yoga occurs

	Venus	Sun Mercury	Rahu
Mars Jupiter	**Chart 8** June 1, 1926		Lagna
Moon			
Ketu		Saturn (R)	

Rahu
2
5
6
Lagna
3
Sun
Mer
4
Saturn (R) 7
1
Venus
10
8
Moon
12
9
11
Mars
Jupiter
Ketu

Lagna	20°15'	Mars	27°54'	Venus	05°55'
Sun	17°37'	Mercury	13°57'	Saturn (R)	28°37'
Moon	26°16'	Jupiter	04°00'	Rahu	24°04'

		Mercury Venus Rahu	Sun Mars Sat (R)
	Navamsha		
Lagna			Moon
	Jupiter Ketu		

8
11
12
Lagna
9
Jupiter
Ketu
10
1
7
4
2
Mer
Venus
Rahu
3
6
5
Sun Mars
Saturn (R)
Moon

Jupiter		Moon Mercury Venus	Sun
Rahu	**Dashamsha**		Saturn (R)
			Ketu
	Mars		Lagna

8 Mars 7
Lagna
Ketu 4 5 Saturn (R)
6 9 3 12
Sun
2 Moon Mercury Venus 1
10 11 Rahu
Jupiter

Lagna	Venus		Saturn (R)
Jupiter Rahu	**Drekkana**		
			Ketu
		Mars	Sun Moon Mercury

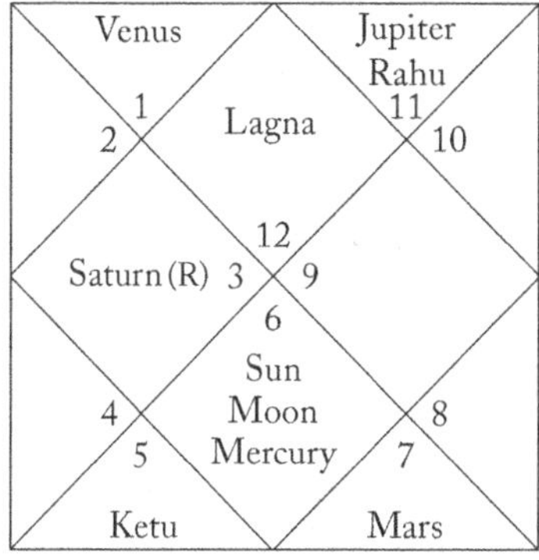

in the eighth house of scandals and intrigues, and that is a big difference when we compare this chart with the previous one. Besides, the Moon, the lagna lord, does not join this combination. The Moon is located in the seventh house. We do not hold the Moon in the seventh house any good for healthy sexual relationships. In addition, an afflicted Venus is also not conducive to a clean sexual image. It will be noted that in the navamsha chart, which is especially relevant to sexual and marital issues, the seventh lord of the lagna chart and the lagna and seventh lords of the navamsha chart, are under affliction as is Venus. The native, an actress, model and singer, was a major sex symbol, and a celebrity for that reason. She had numerous relationships and at least three marriages and divorces. Her prominent raja-yoga ensured that she had relationships with people in high positions. She had been rumoured to be close to even John F. Kennedy and his brother. She had a longstanding dependence on drugs and alcohol. While she was declared as having committed suicide by drug overdose in the early hours of August 5, 1962, theories of conspiracy and intrigue abound till today, and certainly not without merit. There was a feeling that she was intimate with the two Kennedy brothers and that they were instrumental in her death. She was apparently privy to several secrets about the Kennedys and their underworld connections and could pose a danger for them if she ever revealed these!

The dasha at the time of her death was Jupiter-Mars (w.e.f. July 16, 1962). Both the MD and AD lords are in the eighth house of death. The drekkana chart too is important here. The raja-yoga that gave her such prominence in life was as much effective in her death too.

यदि केन्द्रे त्रिकोणे वा निवसेतां तमोग्रहौ ।
नाथेनान्यतरेणापि सम्बन्धाद्योगकारकौ ॥ 21 ॥

21. Rahu and Ketu when located in a kendra or a trikona, and related with another trikona or kendra lord, become yogakarakas.

Comments: Rahu and Ketu do not own any rashis. However, they are capable of giving raja-yoga effects under certain situations. These are:

1. Rahu or Ketu in lagna, associated with a kendra or a trikona lord;
2. Rahu or Ketu in a kendra associated with a trikona lord; and
3. Rahu or ketu in a trikona associated with a kendra lord.

A raja-yoga is formed when a kendra lord and a trikona lord associate with each other. According to this shloka, Rahu or Ketu in a kendra form a good yoga by associating with a trikona lord. They also form a good yoga by being in a trikona and associating with a kendra lord. This is a confirmation of our concept that Rahu and Ketu behave as lords of the houses they occupy. They behave as a kendra lord when in a kendra, and form a raja yoga with a trikona lord. Similarly, they behave as a trikona lord when in a trikona, and form a raja yoga with a kendra lord. Since the lagna is both a kendra and a trikona, their association with another kendra lord or a trikona lord in the lagna would constitute a raja-yoga. It is our opinion that they also yield some good results when they associate with a kendra lord in a kendra or a trikona lord in a trikona although the resulting yoga would be a weak raja-yoga.

Chart 9 (female native, born on July 1, 1961 at 19:45 hours, in Sandringham, England) shows how a raja-yoga links a native to the royal family. It belongs to the late Princess Diana. She has Rahu in the tenth house, a kendra, associated with Mars, the lagna lord. Rahu thus qualifies for a yoga-karaka. Similarly, Ketu in the fourth house, a kendra, is associated with the Moon, the ninth lord. Hence Ketu too qualifies to be a yoga-karaka.

It was in November 1980, during the dasha of Rahu-Moon (from July 19, 1979 to January 17, 1981) that she first met Prince Charles, the heir to the British throne. Rahu is a yoga-karaka graha and the Moon is the ninth lord, another yoga-karaka. Charles was the person she already idolized. They got married on July 29, 1981 during the dasha of Rahu-Mars (from January 17, 1981 to February 4, 1982). Rahu-Mars forms a raja-yoga in the tenth house. It must be noted that it is only the unblemished raja-yogas that give totally unblemished results. Blemished rajayogas suffer the affliction indicated by the house lordship of its constituent

		Venus	Sun Mer (R)
Moon Ketu	**Chart 9 (F)** July 1, 1961		
Sat (R) Jup (R)			Mars Rahu
	Lagna		

10
Sat (R)
Jup (R)
9
Lagna
7
6
Moon
Ketu
8
11
5
2
Mars
Rahu
12
Venus
4
1
3
Sun
Mercury (R)

Lagna	25°06'	Mars	08°19'	Venus	01°04'
Sun	16°20'	Mercury (R)	09°53'	Saturn (R)	04°29'
Moon	01°43'	Jupiter (R)	11°46'	Rahu	04°51'

	Jupiter (R)	Rahu	Mars
Lagna Sun Sat (R)	**Navamsha**		
Venus			
Mer (R)	Ketu	Moon	

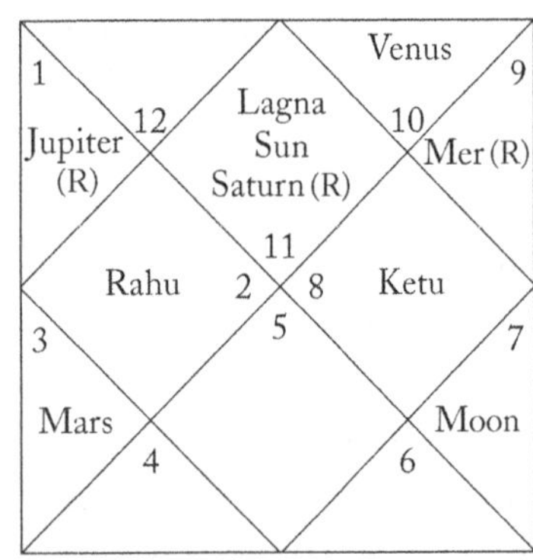

		Jup (R) Venus	Mer (R)
Moon Ketu	**Drekkana**		Lagna
Saturn (R)			Mars Rahu
		Sun	

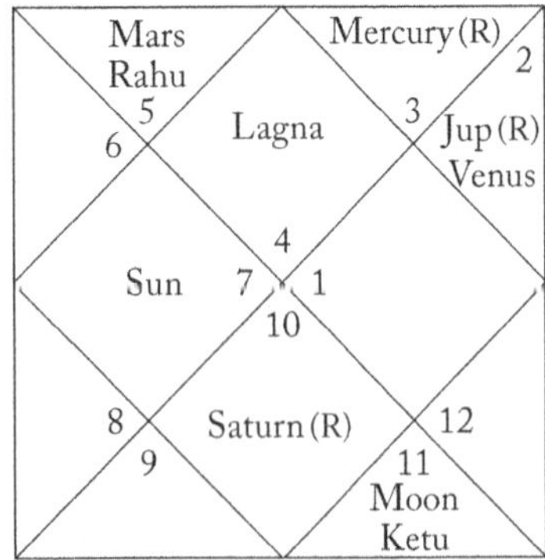

grahas. For Vrishchika lagna, Mars has the blemish of the sixth lordship as well. It is important to take note of such factors too. The chart does harbour promise of marital discord which surfaced soon after marriage. She managed to divert her energies to public life, made a name in the world of fashion, reached out to people, showed empathy for the sick and dying and participated in charities and other functions. She became a darling of the public. The raja-yogas in her chart gave her the prominence that started eclipsing her husband's popularity too. The betrayal by her husband, however, prompted her to delve into several sexual misadventures. Without going into details of the intervening dashas, suffice it to say that the couple divorced officially on August 28, 1996. The dasha running at that time was Jupiter-Rahu (from November 9, 1995 to February 4, 1998). Jupiter is the debilitated retrograde lord of the fifth house (fascination) associating with a malefic retrograde Saturn, and Rahu, the raja-yoga giving graha, along with another natural malefic, Mars, is located in the eighth from the MD lord Jupiter. During the same dasha of Jupiter-Rahu, she died in a car crash along with her then boyfriend Dodi Fayed, the son of a billionaire, on August 31, 1997. The raja-yoga is formed by the sixth lord Mars (both sixth house and Mars stand for accidents) and falls in the eighth house (of death) from the MD lord. Raja-yogas give prominence to the individual. Their quality is tinged by the additional qualifications that attend upon the constituents of the yoga. Please see the drekkana chart to see additional maleficence of the dasha lords; Jupiter is the lord of the sixth house there and the RKA involves the lagna lord occupying the twenty-second drekkana.

धर्मकर्माधिनेतारौ रन्ध्रलाभाधिपौ यदि ।
तयोः सम्बन्धमात्रेण न योगं लभते नरः ॥ 22 ॥

22. If the lords of the ninth and the tenth houses also own the eighth or the eleventh, their mere mutual relationship does not produce yoga for the native.

Comments: It is stated here that a mere relationship between the ninth and the tenth lords, lords of the strongest trikona and the strongest kendra, does not produce yoga if they happen to also own the eighth or the eleventh house. We have been earlier told that any relationship of a trikona lord with a kendra lord would produce yoga. The exception stated here is the additional lordship of the eighth house and the eleventh house. Taking this dictum literally, the situation can apply to the Mesha and Mithuna lagnas. For Mesha lagna, a mere mutual relationship between the ninth lord Jupiter with the tenth lord Saturn would fail to produce yoga because Saturn additionally owns the eleventh house. Equally so, for Mithuna lagna, the mere mutual relationship between the tenth lord Jupiter with the ninth lord Saturn would not produce yoga because Saturn additionally owns the eighth house. By 'mere mutual relationship', it is probably indicated that if there were additional benevolent influences on the yoga, the results would tend to improve.

Chart 10 (male native, born on December 19, 1960 at 13:30 hours in Lucknow, UP, India) belongs to a native with Mesha lagna. Jupiter and Saturn, the ninth and the tenth lords, occupy the ninth house. They are additionally associated with the fourth lord Moon and another trikona lord, the fifth lord Sun. The Saturn-Jupiter yoga thus gets vastly modified. This combination is additionally aspected by the lagna lord Mars from the third house. The native's Rahu dasha runs from January 1, 1999 to December 31, 2016, followed by the dasha of Jupiter, the

	Lagna		Mars (R)
Ketu	**Chart 10 (M)** December 19, 1960		
Venus			Rahu
Sun Moon Jupiter Saturn	Mercury		

3
Mars (R)
2
Lagna
12
11
Ketu
1
4
10
Venus
7
5
Rahu
9
Sun Mon Jup Sat
6
8
Mercury

Lagna	02°31'	Mars (R)	19°44'	Venus	17°17'
Sun	04°07'	Mercury	24°17'	Saturn	24°48'
Moon	16°38'	Jupiter	17°51'	Rahu	15°40'

Mars (R)	Lagna	Sun	Venus
Mercury Ketu	**Navamsha**		
			Moon Rahu
	Saturn		Jupiter

Sun
Mars (R)
3
11
2
Venus
Lagna
12
Mer Ketu
1
4
10
7
5
Moon Rahu
9
6
8
Jupiter
Saturn

Mercury	Lagna	Moon Jupiter	
Venus	**Dashamsha**		Ketu
Sun Rahu			Saturn
Mars (R)			

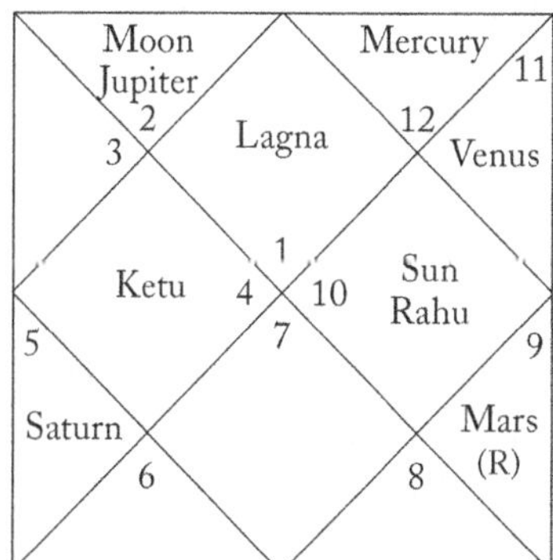

ninth lord. Both Rahu and Jupiter dashas have seen the native enjoy significant professional rise and elevation. Rahu in the fifth house is aspected by the ninth lord Jupiter and its dispositor, the Sun, occupies the ninth house in association with the fourth, the ninth and the tenth lords. The lordship of adverse houses has also affected the results. The native lost his father not too long after the commencement of the Jupiter dasha, after a prolonged illness, and has had troubles with his siblings. However, professionally, the dashas have been satisfactory. It may be noted that all the grahas (except Rahu and Ketu) as well as the lagna are under the influence of Mars: they are either in the signs of Mars or under the aspect of Mars. This signifies a lot of inherent physical and mental energy in the disposition of the native.

The terms used in the shloka are 'dharma' and 'karma' signifying the ninth and the tenth houses. However, in this text the ninth house has been considered as representative of the trikonas and the tenth house of the kendras. The implied meaning of this shloka would then be like this: If the lords of the kendras and the trikonas also happen to own either the eighth house or any of the houses 3, 6 and 11, their mere mutual relationship does not produce yoga for the native. For a yoga to fructify, there must be sufficient additional benefic factors to neutralize the blemishes of the eighth lordship on the one hand and the tri-shad-aaya lordship (lordship of houses 3, 6, 11) on the other. Even then, the yoga would be tinged by the adverse house lords. A good example for study would be the chart of India's late Prime Minister Rajiv Gandhi (**Chart 11,** born on August 20, 1944, at 8:11 hours wartime, at Mumbai, Maharashtra, India). He has a vargottama Simha lagna with the lord of the lagna, the Sun, in the lagna itself. When the lagna of the navamsha chart is the same as that of the rashi chart, it is called as vargottama.

			Saturn
	Chart 11 (M)		Rahu
Ketu	August 20, 1944		Lagna SunMon Mer Ven Jup
			Mars

Mars
Rahu
3
Lagna
Sun Moon
Mer Ven Jup
6
7
4
Saturn
5
8
2
11
9
1
10
12
Ketu

Lagna	14°36'	Mars	01°11'	Venus	18°39'
Sun	03°49'	Mercury	28°34'	Saturn	14°13'
Moon	17°09'	Jupiter	12°12'	Rahu	04°24'

		Sun	
Saturn Ketu	**Navamsha**		Jupiter
Mars			Lagna Rahu
Mercury			Moon Venus

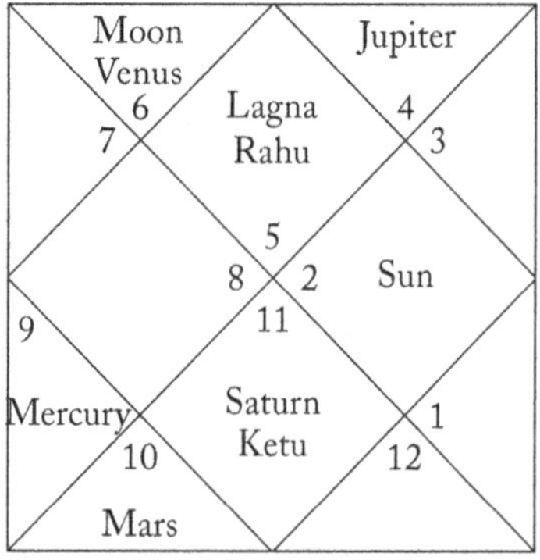

	Rahu	Mars Mercury	
Venus	**Dashamsha**		
Moon			
Lagna Jupiter		Saturn Ketu	Sun

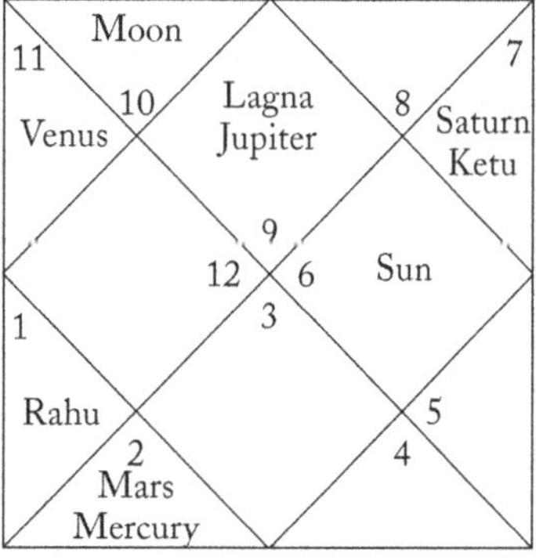

Being vargottama is a state of strength for the lagna as well as for any graha which acquires that qualification. In addition, there are in the lagna the fifth lord Jupiter, the tenth lord Venus, along with the Moon, which is the twelfth lord, and Mercury which owns the second and the eleventh houses. Jupiter additionally owns the eighth house and Venus additionally owns the third house. This combination in the lagna is aspected by Saturn, the sixth and the seventh lord. There are thus strong raja yogas in the lagna blemished by all the adverse lordships of the yoga causing grahas. There is the influence of the tri-shad-aaya house lords as well as the eighth lord. A strong raja yoga which fructified with the death of his mother ultimately ended with the native's own death. The element of accident or trauma, signified by the aspect of the sixth lord Saturn, and that of death, signified by the eighth lord Jupiter, tarnishes such a powerful rajayoga in the lagna. With so many grahas concentrated in the lagna, that too including the lagna lord and all the natural benefics, there was actually too much positive energy concentrated in the lagna. One must also take note of the Gaja-Kesari yoga that obtains in the lagna because of the Moon-Jupiter conjunction, additionally under the influence of several other natural benefics.

The native had a charming personality. His intentions too appear to have been benign. However, at the same time, this concentration in the lagna is at the cost of other houses of the chart. So much concentration of energy in one house causes an imbalance. The circumstances suddenly catapulted him to a position of immense prominence and the eventual fall was equally catastrophic. When the grahas are more evenly distributed in the horoscope, there is more balance in life with no too acute incidences of rise and fall.

Pitfalls in the Interpretation of Yogas

The presence of benefic yogas in the chart indicates a high status for the individual. How high the status depends on many factors which all need to be taken into consideration before pronouncing any results. The same yoga obtaining in different charts will produce different results because of the different qualifications that the yoga may be subject to in different charts. While hundreds of yogas find mention in astrological classics, we are primarily concerned here with the yogas which depend upon the house lordship of grahas. These yogas result from the mutual interaction between different house lords. The house lordship depends upon the rashi falling in the lagna. Thus the same raja yoga which results from the combination of a kendra lord and a trikona lord gives different results in different charts because its constituent grahas are different. In addition, there can be additional different associations or aspects on the yoga-forming grahas which significantly modify and alter the results. The major pitfalls that occur in the interpretation of a yoga are the following:

1. ***Literal interpretation:*** The classics mention of results attributed to a yoga in purely black and white terms without mentioning any of the grey shades. The classics make one a king if there is a raja yoga and a pauper if there is an adverse yoga. This applies also to yogas which are not solely dependent on house lordship. It is essential to apply the rules of the classics liberally, not literally.

2. ***Overlooking contrary yogas:*** Results of a yoga only fructify if it is not neutralized completely by another yoga indicating contrary results. Since this classic primarily concerns itself with the presence or absence of raja yogas and does not delve into yogas which deal

with monetary status, penury and ill health, the reader is well advised to refer to the appropriate classics for the same.

3. ***Importance of attending qualifications:*** It is not very common to find a pure yoga in a chart without some attending qualifications. One chart that we have dealt with earlier **(chart 2)**, belonging to Dr Rajendra Prasad, shows an unblemished raja yoga in the lagna aspected by an unblemished lagna lord Jupiter. But it is rare to find such charts in common practice. It is essential that if there is a strong raja yoga in the chart, the weaknesses inherent in that yoga must also be identified. We have already observed in the chart of Rajiv Gandhi above that a highly potent rajayoga in the lagna is blemished by the same grahas which are conferring the rajayoga, because their other house lordship is adverse. Thus there are yoga results as well as the destruction of the yoga.

Factors that determine the outcome of a yoga

In this chapter we have learnt that raja yogas, i.e., yogas that confer social status and professional elevation, result when the kendra and trikona lords get somehow mutually linked. When these yogas are formed only by the grahas which own the kendras and trikonas and no other adverse houses, they confer undiluted and unblemished status, prestige, dignity, benevolence and professional elevation upon the native. Their purity is not affected by the simultaneous lordship of neutral houses, like the second or the twelfth, by their constituent grahas. However, the ownership of house 3, 6, 11 or 8 confers a blemish on the concerned graha which tarnishes the outcome of the yoga. The yoga does fructify but is greatly modified by the attending additional factors. The following factors tend to determine the outcome of a yoga:

1. ***Inherent nature of grahas constituting the yoga:*** The inherent nature of the grahas modifies the results of the yoga, Thus a Mars-Jupiter combination of ninth and tenth lords for Meena lagna would behave differently from a Moon-Sun combination of ninth and tenth lords for Vrishchika lagna.
2. ***Rulership of yoga-forming grahas:*** We have already seen above that grahas give results depending upon their rulership. Venus as the tenth lord for Simha lagna would behave differently from Venus as the tenth lord for Makara lagna because its other house lordship is different.
3. ***Houses involved in the yoga formation:*** A raja yoga formed by the same house lords for the same lagna for two different natives would yield different results depending upon the houses in which the yoga forms in the two charts. We have seen this in **charts 7 and 8** discussed earlier. In one case the Mars-Jupiter combination for Karka lagna falls in the ninth house while in the other it falls in the eighth house, with markedly different results.
4. ***Strength of the constituent grahas:*** The inherent strength of the grahas that constitute a yoga determines to a large extent the degree to which a yoga would yield its results. A yoga formed by grahas which are located in their own houses or in their moolatrikonas or in exaltation or in strength in the navamsha chart yields far superior results to the one formed by weak, debilitated or combust grahas.
5. ***Modifying factors:*** These include association or aspect of other grahas on the yoga-forming grahas, or even the nature of rashis in which a yoga forms.
6. ***Appropriate dasha order:*** In order that one gets the full benefit of a rajayoga (or any other yoga for that matter),

it is essential that an appropriate dasha operates at an appropriate time. The dasha order determines when and how the promise inherent in a chart is enjoyed or suffered by the native.

Adverse houses and raja-yoags

We have learnt above that houses 3, 6, 11 and 8 are adverse houses. Even the twelfth house, which is the house indicating losses, is considered adverse by the classics. The appropriate astrological term for houses 6, 8 and 12 is 'Trika'. The Trika houses and their lords are supposed to yield adverse results during their dasha and they tend to blemish any other grahas that they associate with. Sage Parashara, however, mentions of some raja-yogas which may result in relation to such adverse houses or their lords. Some of such yogas are as follows:

1. Natural malefics in houses 3 and 6 confer raja yoga on the native;
2. Debilitated grahas in houses 3, 6 or 8 with the lagna lord either exalted or in its own house and aspecting the lagna;
3. Lord of house 6, 8 or 12 debilitated, combust or in an inimical rashi, and lagna lord in its own house or in exaltation aspecting the lagna;
4. Debilitated lords of houses 6, 8 and 12 cause a raja yoga if they also aspect the lagna; and
5. Debilitated grahas in houses 3, 6, 8 or 11 cause raja yoga if they also aspect the lagna.

Note: It may be noted here that, although the classic mentions it, no grahas can aspect the lagna from houses 3 and 8. Only Mars and Saturn can aspect the lagna from the 6th and 11th houses respectively. If partial aspects are considered, all grahas can aspect the lagna from houses 6 and 11. However, partial aspects are not considered in the *Laghu Parashari*. These aspects are possible if we consider the Jaimini aspects. However, our classic is strictly restricted to the Parashari principles.

Another category of rajayogas of an odd nature results from the specific disposition of the lords of the sixth, eighth and twelfth houses. They are called as the ***Vipareeta rajayogas***. Three types of such yogas result when;

1. The sixth lord occupies the eighth or the twelfth house (Harsha yoga);
2. The eighth lord occupies the sixth or the twelfth house (Sarala yoga); or
3. The twelfth lord occupies the sixth or the eighth house (Vimala yoga).

All these yogas are supposed to ensure rise in status, fame and financial gains during the dashas of the grahas that constitute these yogas.

Let us see how these yogas work in actual practice. **Chart 12** (August 4, 1961, at 19:24 hours, in Honolulu, Hawaii, USA) belongs to Barack Obama, the erstwhile US

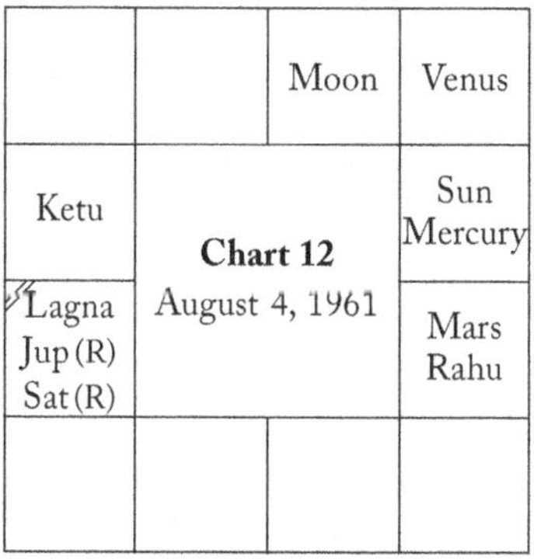

		Moon	Venus
Ketu	**Chart 12** August 4, 1961		Sun Mercury
Lagna Jup (R) Sat (R)			Mars Rahu

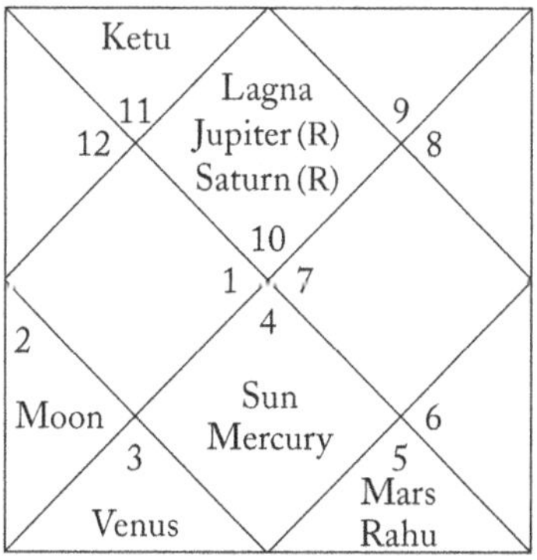

Ketu
11
12
Lagna
Jupiter (R)
Saturn (R)
9
8
10
1
7
4
2
Moon
Sun
Mercury
6
3
5
Mars
Rahu
Venus

Lagna	24°43'	Mars	29°15'	Venus	08°28'
Sun	19°13'	Mercury	09°00'	Saturn (R)	02°00'
Moon	10°02'	Jupiter (R)	07°32'	Rahu	03°59'

Jupiter (R)	Moon	Rahu	
	Navamsha		
Saturn (R)			Lagna
Sun Mars Venus	Ketu		Mercury

Mercury
6
7
Lagna
4
3
5
Ketu 8
2 Rahu
11
9 Sun Mars Venus
1
Moon
10
12
Saturn (R)
Jupiter (R)

Ketu	Moon	Lagna Mars	Mercury
	Dashamsha		
			Venus
	Jup (R)		Sun Sat (R) Rahu

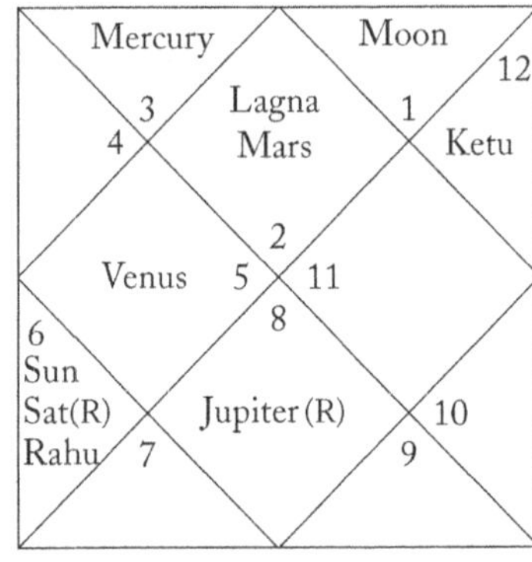

President. His chart shows a debilitated twelfth lord Jupiter with the lagna lord Saturn in its own house in the lagna. Thus we have a debilitated lord of the twelfth house, and a strong lagna lord which occupies the lagna itself. This fulfills the condition for a rajayoga. Another condition which is fulfilled is that there is a debilitated twelfth lord in the lagna. Jupiter in the lagna is also subject to cancellation of its debilitation because of its association with Saturn; this situation itself goes by the name 'Neecha-Bhanga rajayoga', i.e., a rajayoga which is caused by the cancellation of debilitation. It was in the dasha of Jupiter-Moon (from November 23, 2007 to March 24, 2009) that the native was nominated as US Presidential candidate, won the Presidential election and finally joined office of

President of the USA. The Moon is thc exalted seventh lord. The seventh lord indicates, according to sage Parashara, *Padonnati* (पदोन्नति) or rise in official status. After four years, he was reelected to the high office in November 2012. By then the dasha of the lagna lord Saturn in the lagna, associated with a raja-yoga-karaka Jupiter, had commenced.

CHAPTER 4

मारकाध्यायः

Concerning Longevity

अष्टमं ह्यायुषः स्थानमष्टमादष्टमं च यत्।
तयोरपि व्ययस्थानं मारकस्थानमुच्यते ॥23॥

23. The eighth (from the lagna) is verily the house for longevity as is also the eighth from the eighth (i.e., the third from the lagna). Twelfth from each of these (i.e., the seventh and the second from the lagna) is called as the maraka ('killer') house.

Comments: This chapter concerns itself with the grahas that indicate the end of life. The end of life would naturally be related to the longevity of the native. The dashas of the maraka, or 'killer', grahas would precipitate the event of death when the longevity of the individual is over. This consequently leads us to the determination of longevity before deciding on the killer dashas. The killer dashas would operate several times during the lifetime of the native but would cause death only when the longevity is over. The classics also advocate that no great raja yoga or dhana yoga (combination for wealth) should be pronounced by an astrologer without first determining the longevity of the native. If the native is not going to enjoy sufficient length of life, any great yogas in the chart become irrelevant.

It may be emphasized that determination of longevity is not an easy task. It needs all the skills of a proficient astrologer to be able to come close to the exact span of life. There are so many principles described about the calculation of longevity in the classics that one tends to get lost in them. Still some rough assessment about the likely lifespan of the native must be made before reaching any sound conclusion about the results of any yogas present in the chart.

The classics describe the following categories in which the span of life may be judged:

1. Balarishta: Up to the age of eight years;
2. Yogarishta: Eight to twenty years;
3. Alpaayu: Short life, till 33 years;
4. Madhyaayu: Medium lifespan, up to 66 years (70 years according to some);
5. Poornaayu: Long life, till a hundred (or one hundred and twenty) years;
6. Divyaayu: Divine lifespan; a thousand years;
7. Amitaayu: Over a thousand years.

Balarishta, or suffering during early years, is a subject which has been dealt with in some details by most classics. Standard astrological principles indicate whether or not a child would suffer during childhood. The classics mostly pronounce death to the child in most cases if the Balarishta combinations exist in the chart. We have emphasized on several occasions other than in this classic that these principles need highly judicious application. Sage Parashara also advocates that one should not predict in any detail about a native below the age of twelve. The sage says that a child up to the age of twelve can die because of the Paapa-Karmas (sinful deeds) of his mother or of his father or his own

Paapa-Karmas committed during the previous births and these may not show appreciably in the horoscopic chart. In such a situation, any fanciful predictions would be irrelevant.

Between the ages of eight and twenty, no standard principles about longevity are available. Yogas are mentioned in the classics indicating specific lifespans for the natives in whose charts such yogas are present. However, well laid down principles are not there. One needs a careful application of his understanding of astrology to unearth likely adverse events in this category of natives.

Divyaayu and Amitaayu are not for the normal individuals and we need not go into those areas. As far as the determination of longevity for normal individuals is concerned, there are numerous methods available in the classics. The availability of several methods only indicates that none of these can be relied upon in all cases. There are some methods of mathematical calculation of longevity for normal individuals. These methods give good results only sometimes while they fail miserably in several other cases. We would not totally discard them as they incorporate some of the very sound principles of Vedic astrology. However, they miss something and that renders them often unreliable for general use. We shall, however, try to discuss some principles from the classics which are reasonably reliable in most cases. For that purpose, we would consider three spans of life: short life (Alpaayu), medium life (Madhyaayu) and long life (Poornaayu). Assuming that the lifespan of most individuals qualifying for long life would extend to a maximum of a hundred years, we have roughly divided this length of time into three parts. Thus short life may be taken to go up to thirty-three years or around that, a medium lifespan would mean something like thirty-three to sixty-six years and a long lifespan would extend to a hundred years. The reader need not stick to this exact division and may change this to suit his understanding.

Determination of Longevity

Three groups of factors need to be taken into consideration:

Group I	(a) Lagna lord, and	(b) the eighth lord
Group II	(a) Lagna, and	(b) the Moon
Group III	(a) Lagna, and	(b) the Hora lagna

In each of the three groups above, there are two components, (a) and (b). The placement of each of these two components, for each of the three groups, eventually decides the span of life an individual would fall into, thus:

1. If both (a) and (b) fall into Chara rashis: Poornaayu
2. If both fall into Sthira rashis: Alpaayu
3. If both in Dwiswabhava rashis: Madhyaayu
4. One in Chara and the other in Sthira: Madhyaayu
5. One in Chara, other in Dwiswabhava: Alpaayu
6. One in Sthira, other in Dwiswabhava: Poornaayu

If all three groups or any two of the three groups indicate the same span of life, that should be accepted. In case the three groups indicate different spans of life, consider the one indicated by Group III (i.e., lagna and Hora lagna). In case the three groups indicate different lifespans but there is the Moon in the lagna or the seventh house, consider the lifespan indicated by Group II (i.e., lagna and the Moon).

Note: For Group II above, sage Parashara considers Saturn and the Moon instead of the lagna and the Moon. We have taken the above concept from sage Jaimini and this seems to give better results.

Determination of the Hora lagna

The Hora lagna for the purpose of determination of longevity needs to be arrived at as follows:

Step I Find out the number of hours and minutes that have elapsed from the time of sunrise to the time of birth of the native.

Step II Consider the hours as rashis (subtract 12 if the number exceeds 12 and consider the remainder). Divide the minutes by two; this gives the degrees. The rashis and degrees may be considered as the Ishta-Kaala (IK).

Step III Obtain the Hora lagna thus:

(a) If the lagna is an even rashi, add the IK to the sign and degree of the lagna.

(b) If the lagna is odd, add the IK to the longitude of the Sun.

For making the above principles clear, we shall consider an example here. Let us consider a native (**Chart 13**) born on March 6, 1949 at 01:05 hours IST in Delhi (India). The natal lagna is Vrishchika. Let us first of all arrive at the Hora lagna. Since he was born on March 6, 1949 before sunrise, we need to take the sunrise on the previous day, i.e., on March 5, 1949.

	hrs.	min.	sec.
Time of birth March 6, 1949	25	05	00
Sunrise on March 5, 1949 in Delhi	− 6	47	40
Time of birth since sunrise	18	17	20

Since each hour is equivalent to one rashi, 18 hours give us **6 rashis** (after subtracting 12). Every two minutes are equivalent to one degree. Thus we get **8°40'** from 17 minutes and 20 seconds. Hence the Ishta-Kaala is **6^{s}8°40'**.

Since the lagna here is even, we add the IK to the lagna.

Ishta-Kaala		$06^{s}08°40'00''$
Lagna	+	$07^{s}19°31'30''$
Hora Lagna	=	$13^{s}28°11'30''$, i.e., **$1^{s}28°11'30''$**.

That is, **Hora Lagna is Vrisha 28°11'30"**.

	Moon Rahu		
Sun Mars Venus	**Chart 13** March 6, 1949		
Mercury Jupiter			Saturn (R)
	Lagna	Ketu	

Ketu
10
9
Mer Jup
Lagna
7
6
Sun Mars Venus
8
11
5
Saturn (R)
2
12
4
1
3
Moon Rahu

Lagna	19°31'	Mars	24°15'	Venus	11°06'
Sun	21°46'	Mercury	25°24'	Saturn (R)	08°41'
Moon	26°22'	Jupiter	01°05'	Rahu	03°09'

	Sun Rahu	Mars	Jupiter (R)
	Navamsha		
Jupiter Venus			Mercury
Lagna	Moon	Ketu	

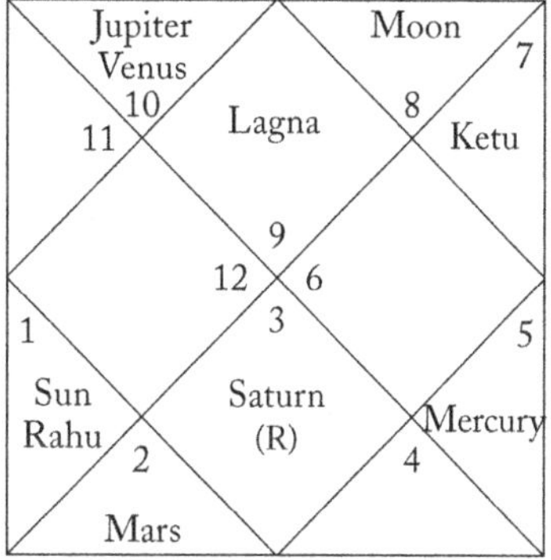

Lagna	Rahu		Venus
	Drekkana		
Jupiter			Saturn (R)
Moon		Sun Mars Ketu	Mercury

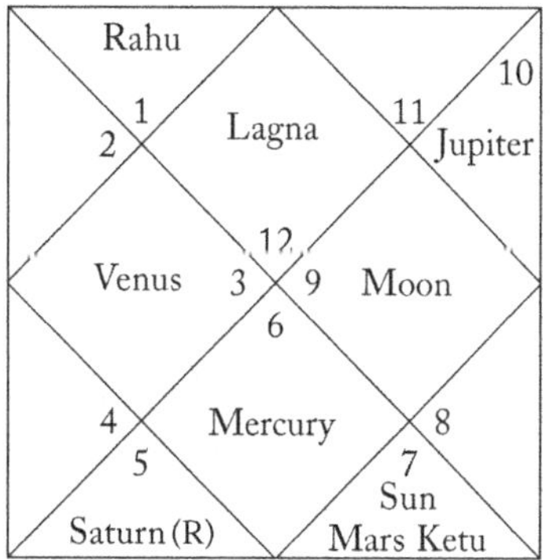

		Rahu	Lagna Venus
Moon	**Dwadashamsha**		
Jupiter			
	Mars Mer Sat(R) Ketu	Sun	

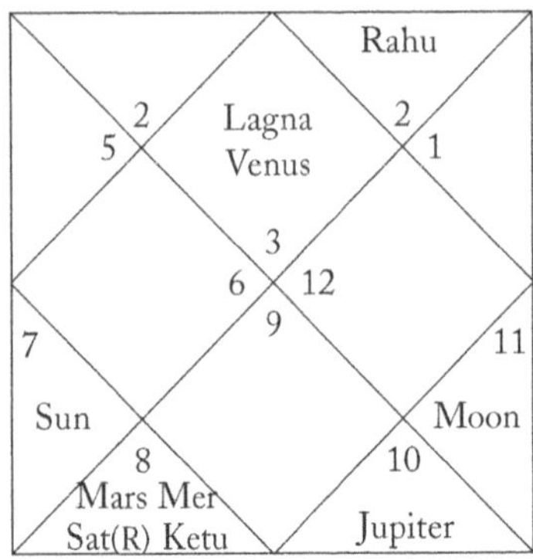

Let us now determine the lifespan in which the native would likely fall.

Group I	Lagna lord Mars in Kumbha:	Sthira
	Eighth lord Mercury in Makara:	Chara
	Result:	Madhyaayu
Group II	Lagna Vrishchika:	Sthira
	Moon in Mesha:	Chara
	Result:	Madhyaayu
Group III	Lagna Vrishchika:	Sthira
	Hora Lagna Vrisha:	Sthira
	Result:	Alpaayu

Since out of the three groups, we get Madhyaayu in two groups, we accept this and, therefore, the native belongs to the Madhyaayu group. He died on February 1, 2015, at the age of sixty-five, because of myocardial infarction (heart attack) when he was running the dasha of Saturn-Venus. Venus is the maraka seventh lord. Saturn too qualifies as a killer as we shall learn later (shloka 28).

We must warn here that the method described above is not fool proof. It applies eminently to the chart under consideration but this is not the rule. The reader must take several precautions before putting any one method to general use.

Another method prescribed by Mantreshwara, the author of the *Phaladeepika*, another standard text on Vedic astrology, is being given here. Consider three groups and get the mean of what you eventually get as the result.

Group I Drekkana sign of (a) lagna and (b) the Moon;

Group II Navamsha sign of (a) lagna lord and (b) the Moon sign lord;

Group III Dwadashamsha sign of (a) lagna lord and (b) the eighth lord.

Let us apply the above principles to the chart of the native under consideration. His drekkana lagna and the Moon fall in Dwiswabhava rashis indicating Madhyaayu. See the drekkana chart above to see this.

His lagna lord as well as his Moon sign lord is Mars, in a fixed sign in navamsha indicating Alpaayu.

His lagna lord Mars and the eighth lord Mercury in the dwadashamsha fall together in Vrishchika, a fixed sign, again indicating Alpaayu.

So we get Madhyaayu, Alpaayu and Alpaayu. An average of the three indicates the lifespan granted to him. Thus we see that different methods give different results and we should not depend on only one method.

There are some additional principles which also must be taken into account while deciding on the longevity of a native. Some of the combinations indicating various lifespans are as follows:

1. All benefics in kendras: Poornaayu
2. All benefics in panapharas: Madhyaayu
3. All benefics in apoklimas: Alpaayu
4. Eighth lord and all malefics in kendras: Alpaayu
5. Eighth lord and all malefics in panapharas: Madhyaayu

6. Eighth lord and all malefics in apoklimas: Poornaayu
7. Strong lagna lord, benefics in kendras and malefics in houses 3, 6, 11: Poornaayu
8. Stronger of the lagna lord and the eighth lord
   (a) In a kendra: Poornaayu
   (b) In a panaphara: Madhaayu
   (c) In an apoklima: Alpaayu
9. Lagna lord and the eighth lord located
   (a) In their own houses: Poornaayu
   (b) In the houses of their neutrals: Madhyaayu
   (c) In the houses of their enemies: Alpaayu
10. Weak lagna lord in house 6, 8 or 12, bereft of benefic aspect: Alpaayu
11. Malefics in kendras, bereft of benefic aspect, and a weak lagna lord: Alpaayu
12. Malefics in houses 2 and 12, without any benefic aspect: Alpaayu

Once the astrologer has some idea of the category of the lifespan a native falls in, he should analyse the maraka dashas operating around the likely time of conclusion of longevity according to the principles described further in this text. We do not want to go into any further elaborate methods of calculation of longevity. For further study, the reader is advised to refer to the several available classics which deal with longevity calculation. It may, however, be pointed out here that while maraka dashas do indicate death, they only kill when the lifespan is over. At other times, they have the potential to disturb health. The above narration only gives an idea of the slot of lifespan a native would fall into. People do not die at the fixed ages of 33 or 66 or 100. A deep analysis is required to get nearer to the likely longevity of the native.

It is stated in the verse under consideration that the eighth is the house for longevity. The author further states that the eighth from the eighth, i.e., the third from the lagna, is also the house for longevity. This is a standard Parashari principle. If you consider the fifth house for progeny, fifth from the fifth also qualifies to be the house for progeny. The tenth is the house for professional status; tenth from the tenth, i.e., the seventh from the lagna, also indicates professional status. We have already stated that the seventh house is for Padonnati, rise in status! This principle applies to the house of longevity, the eighth house, as well. The author further states that the twelfth from each house of longevity is the maraka house. A 'maraka' is a killer. Twelfth house indicates loss. Twelfth from the house of longevity would indicate loss of longevity, hence death. That is why the seventh and the second houses from the lagna qualify to be maraka houses.

तत्राप्याद्यव्ययस्थानादुत्तरं बलवत्तरम् ।
तदीशितुस्तत्रगताः पापिनस्तेन संयुताः ॥ 24 ॥

तेषां दशाविपाकेषु सम्भवे निधनं नृणाम् ।
तेषामसम्भवे साक्षाद् व्ययाधीशदशास्वपि ॥ 25 ॥

24, 25. Of the maraka houses, the second in order is the stronger one. (When longevity is over), death of an individual is possible during the dasha-antardasha of the lord of a maraka house, of an occupant of the maraka house, or of an associated malefic graha. When that is not possible, the dashas (MD, AD) of the twelfth lord (from the lagna) prove to be marakas.

Comments: The first part of the shloka must be considered along with Shloka 23. As the eighth and the third houses are declared the houses of longevity, the twelfth from the eighth and the twelfth from the third, i.e., houses seven and two, are to be considered as marakas. Of these two maraka houses, the author states that the 'second in order' is the stronger maraka. The second in order of the definition of maraka is the second house from the lagna, the twelfth from the third house. Thus the second house happens to be a bigger maraka than the seventh house. Authorities differ in interpreting the shloka. Some hold that the 'second in order' must be considered as the second maraka house from the lagna. In that case, the seventh house would qualify to be a stronger maraka. In our own view, the shloka conveys that the second house from the lagna is the stronger of the two maraka houses, and in this we have the support of several distinguished scholars.

In the shlokas under consideration, the author indicates the likely dashas and antardashas which may cause the death of the native. These include the dashas and antardashas of:

- The lords of the maraka houses;
- Occupants of the maraka houses;
- Malefics associated with the above.

If death does not result during the dashas indicated, then the dashas and antardashas of the twelfth lord tend to be fatal.

अलाभे पुनरेतेषां सम्बन्धेन व्ययेशितुः ।
क्वचिच्छुभानां च दशास्वष्टमेशदशासु च ॥ 26 ॥

26. In case the earlier mentioned maraka dashas are not available (at the time of conclusion of longevity), death may sometimes occur

> during the dashas of benefics related to the twelfth lord, and during the dashas (MD, AD, PD) of the eighth lord.

Comments: It may be noted that the author does not categorically state that such and such dasha would certainly cause death. He specifies the likely dashas that indicate death. After the second and the seventh houses, which are the primary maraka houses, the author indicates in the previous shloka that the twelfth house may also take up maraka function. In the present shloka, it is indicated that death may be possible in the dasha of a functional benefic also if that benefic happens to be related to the twelfth lord. And next in order comes the eighth lord which we have already known as the worst malefic.

It may be noted that our author mentions of the maraka effects of the eighth lord a little low in order. We have actually noticed this role of the eighth house and the eighth lord rather more often. This happens more often when the dasha of the lagna lord is also involved somehow with the eighth lord dasha. We have earlier noted in **chart 8** belonging to Marilyn Monroe that she died in the dasha of yoga-karaka grahas, Jupiter and Mars, both located in the eighth house. Mars in her case is the yoga-karaka for Karka lagna and Jupiter is the ninth lord in addition to being the sixth lord. The eighth house was involved there although the lagna lord was not directly involved. It has been our observation that even the mutual dasha-antardasha of the lagna lord and the eighth lord quite often proves to be death-inflicting provided there is appropriate indication in the chart. **Chart 14** (male native, born on September 25, 1952, at 3:12 hours, in New York, USA) belongs to Christopher Reeve, the American actor, writer and director

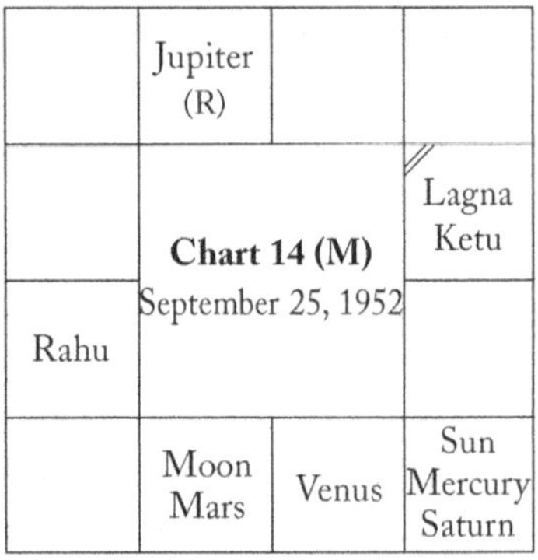

	Jupiter (R)		
	Chart 14 (M) September 25, 1952		Lagna Ketu
Rahu			
	Moon Mars	Venus	Sun Mercury Saturn

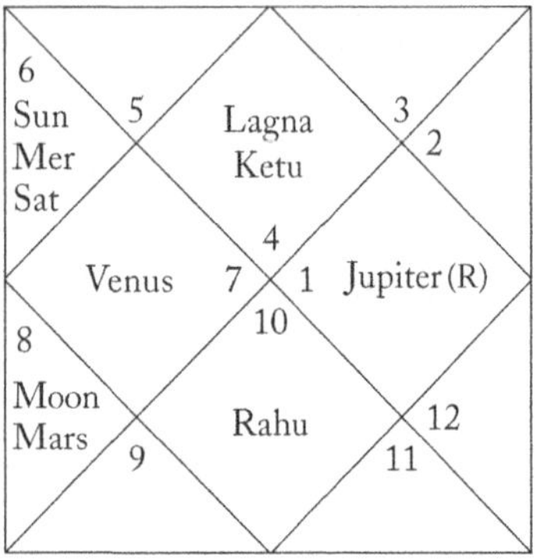

6 Sun Mer Sat
5
Lagna Ketu
3
2
4
Venus
7
1
Jupiter (R)
10
8 Moon Mars
Rahu
12
9
11

Lagna	25°51'	Mars	25°03'	Venus	03°48'
Sun	08°57'	Mercury	09°32'	Saturn	22°48'
Moon	19°20'	Jupiter (R)	27°23'	Rahu	27°48'

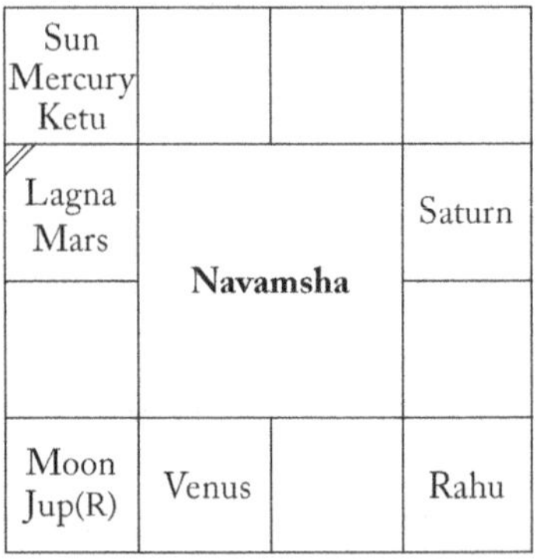

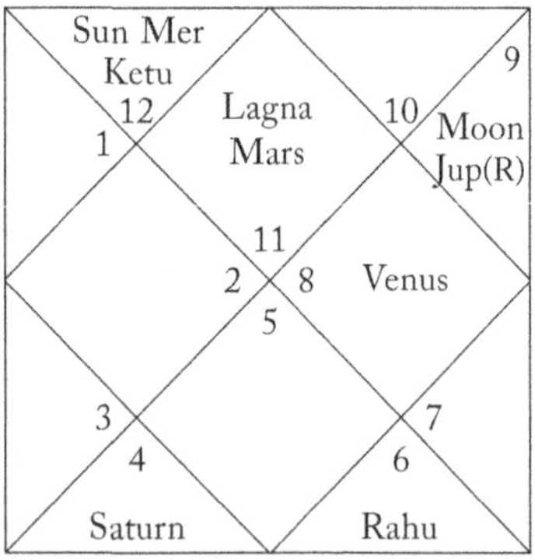

Sun Mercury Ketu			
Lagna Mars	**Navamsha**		Saturn
Moon Jup(R)	Venus		Rahu

Sun Mer Ketu
12
1
Lagna Mars
10
9
Moon Jup(R)
11
2
8
Venus
5
3
4
7
6
Saturn
Rahu

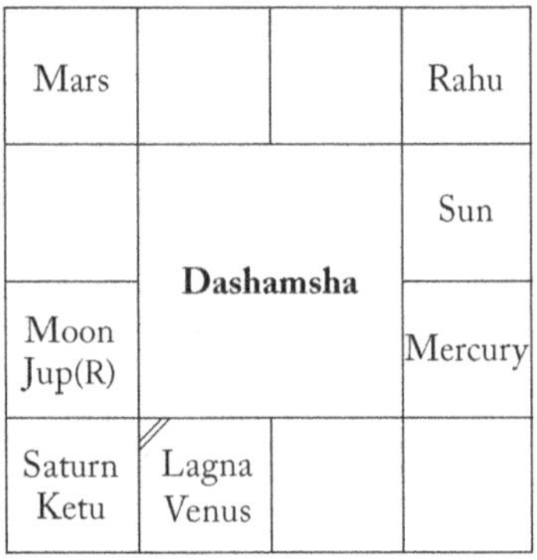

Mars			Rahu
	Dashamsha		Sun
Moon Jup(R)			Mercury
Saturn Ketu	Lagna Venus		

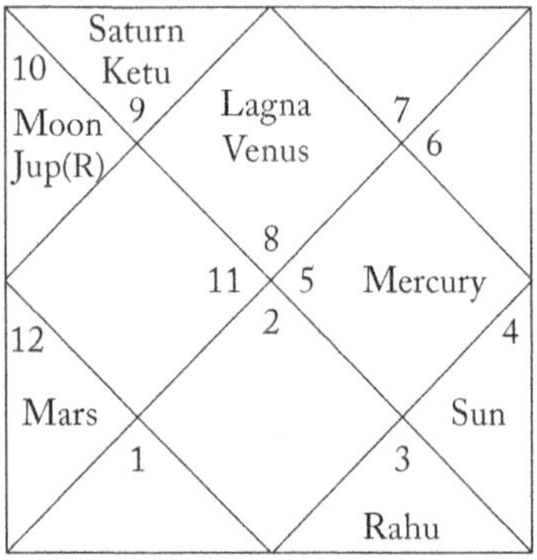

Saturn Ketu
10
9
Moon Jup(R)
Lagna Venus
7
6
8
11
5
Mercury
2
12
4
Mars
Sun
1
3
Rahu

who is more popularly known as '*Superman*' for his role in his highly acclaimed movie of that name. The movie was released in December 1978 when he was running the dasha of Venus-Moon (August 31, 1977 to May 2, 1979). Venus in its own rashi in the fourth house forms a potent raja yoga by being a kendra lord aspected by the ninth lord Jupiter from the tenth house. Venus remains significant for his professional work in the navamsha and dashamsha charts as well. More or less the whole MD of Venus was a professionally and financially remarkable period for him. The other house ruled by Venus is the eleventh which indicates earnings and achievements. We have held here that the eleventh house is the strongest of the adverse houses. Because of the raja-yoga that the kendra lord Venus gives rise to by receiving the ninth lord Jupiter's aspect, besides forming one of the Pancha-Mahapurusha yogas by virtue of being a graha posited in its own house in a kendra, the likely negative effect of eleventh house lordship is more than neutralised. The AD lord Moon is the lagna lord which forms another potent raja-yoga in the fifth house by associating with the yoga-karaka Mars for Karka lagna. Mars also cancels the debilitation of the Moon.

The native suffered a fall while horse riding on May 27, 1995, fracturing his vertebrae in the neck and suffering quadriplegia (paralysis of all four limbs). The dasha running at that time was Sun-Jupiter (May 20, 1995 to March 7, 1996). The Sun is a maraka (lord of the second house) associated with a malefic third (and twelfth) lord Mercury, and a malefic, maraka (seventh and eighth lord) Saturn in the third house (neck, movement). The AD lord was retrograde Jupiter, the sixth lord (accidents). It was an accident during movement, involving the neck. He underwent surgery to fix the broken neck bones soon after and went through rigorous physiotherapy resulting in some significant improvement over the following years. However, he succumbed to an infection from a pressure sore and a cardiac arrest on October 10, 2004 when he was running the dasha of Moon-Saturn (August 1, 2003 to March 1, 2005), the MD of the lagna lord and the AD of the eighth lord. If we go to the next finer division of the dasha, it was the MD-AD-PD of Moon-Saturn-Rahu (from September 18, 2004 to December 14, 2004). Rahu is the occupant of the maraka seventh house, representing the malefic seventh and eighth lord Saturn. It is also noteworthy that the Rahu-Ketu axis is quite close to the degree of the lagna, thus influencing the lagna more intensely.

We are seeing here that the lagna lord which is supposed to be the best benefic can also have its role in death (and disease). The lagna indicates the body of the native. If there is a bad dasha involving the lagna lord, the health and survival of the native can get affected. In **chart 15** (male native, born on April 23, 1937, at 16:39 hours IST, in Delhi, India), the lagna lord Mercury occupies the eighth house along with the lords of two maraka houses, the second lord Venus and the twelfth lord Sun. Here we are considering the Sun also as a maraka lord because our author attributes the maraka function to the twelfth house also when the second and the seventh lords are not available for the maraka role. The native had some cardiac issues for which he had undergone angioplasty sometime in the dasha of Mercury-Sun (March 4, 2009 to January 8, 2010). In cases of heart ailments, an afflicted Sun plays an important role because the Sun is the karaka for the heart.

The patient again needed an angioplasty which was done in a reputed Delhi hospital on October 18, 2012. While the surgery went on well, the native developed some drug reaction in the postoperative period leading to damage to his kidneys, and eventually multi-organ failure, resulting in his death on October 22, 2012. The native was running the dasha of Mercury-Rahu (June 6, 2012 to December 24,

Saturn	Sun Mercury Venus (R)	Ketu	
	Chart 15 (M) April 23, 1937		
Jupiter			
	Mars (R) Rahu		Lagna Moon

8
7
Mars (R)
Rahu
Lagna
Moon
5
4
6
9
3
12
10
2
Jupiter
Saturn
Ketu
11
1
Sun Mer
Venus (R)

Lagna	11°53'	Mars (R)	12°03'	Venus (R)	01°18'
Sun	09°53'	Mercury	29°12'	Saturn	06°48'
Moon	15°49'	Jupiter	03°34'	Rahu	22°54'

	Lagna Venus (R)	Moon	Sun
Jupiter	**Navamsha**		Ketu
Rahu			
Mercury		Mars (R)	Saturn

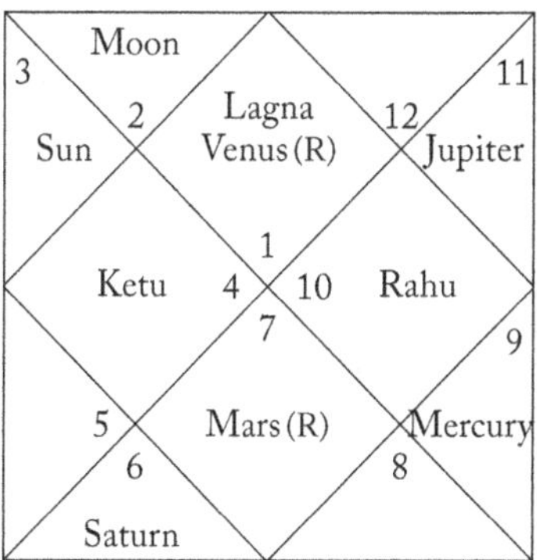

Mars (R) Saturn	Sun Ven (R)		
	Drekkana		Rahu
Lagna Mon Jup Ketu			
Mercury			

Mercury
12
Lagna
Moon
Jupiter
Ketu
11
9
Mars (R)
Sat
8
10
Sun
Venus (R)
1
7
4
2
Rahu
6
3
5

2014) at that time. Mercury is the afflicted lagna lord in the eighth house. The AD lord Rahu is in the third house (eighth from the eighth), associated with the third and the eighth lord Mars. Rahu thus represents the eighth lord Mars only, doubly so because it occupies the house of the eighth lord and also associates with the (retrograde, hence adverse for health) eighth lord. The AD lord is situated in the eighth house from the MD lord. This example only illustrates the adverse role of the mutual MD/AD of grahas related to the lagna and the eighth house. In the drekkana chart too, Mercury and Rahu retain their mutually 6/8 relationship; Mercury owns the adverse sixth house while Rahu involves the lagna in the RKA.

The adverse results associated with the dasha of the lagna lord sometimes also come to the fore during the mutual MD/AD of the lagna and the sixth lords. The lagna lord concerns itself with the health of the individual as we already know. The sixth is the house of disease. If there is sufficient affliction of the sixth lord, its MD or AD can prove adverse for health or survival. The native of **chart 16** (male native, born on October 10, 1950, at 16:05 hours IST in Ludhiana, Punjab, India) was a small time cine artist. He has a conglomeration of six grahas in his eighth house. Natives with several grahas in their eighth house often have hidden talents which come out in the open as appropriate dashas operate and unfold their talents. However, such overcrowding in this adverse house also tends to create health issues. The native had longstanding cardiac problems for which he was under treatment. In the early hours of June 6, 2014, the native suffered a massive heart attack and expired. The operating dasha at that time was Saturn-Moon (July 22, 2013 to February 21, 2015), the lagna lord and the sixth lord, both located in the overcrowded eighth house. Going to the next finer level, it was the MD-AD-PD of Saturn-Moon-Saturn (March 25, 2014 to June 26, 2014).

Rahu			
Lagna Jup (R)	**Chart 16 (M)** October 10, 1950		
	Mars		Sun Mon Mer Ven Sat Ketu

Rahu
12
1
Lagna
Jupiter (R)
10
9
11
2
8
Mars
5
3
4
7
6
Sun Mon
Mer Ven Sat Ketu

Lagna	12°20'	Mars	17°08'	Venus	14°33'
Sun	23°23'	Mercury	08°07'	Saturn	02°30'
Moon	08°05'	Jupiter (R)	04°44'	Rahu	05°11'

Moon Mercury		Venus	
Ketu	**Navamsha**		
Lagna Saturn			Sun Rahu
Mars	Jupiter (R)		

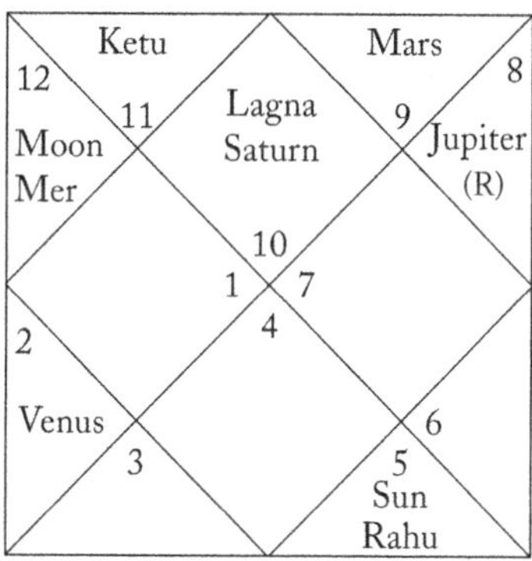

Mars Rahu		Sun	Lagna
Jupiter (R)	**Drekkana**		
Venus			
			Moon Mercury Saturn Ketu

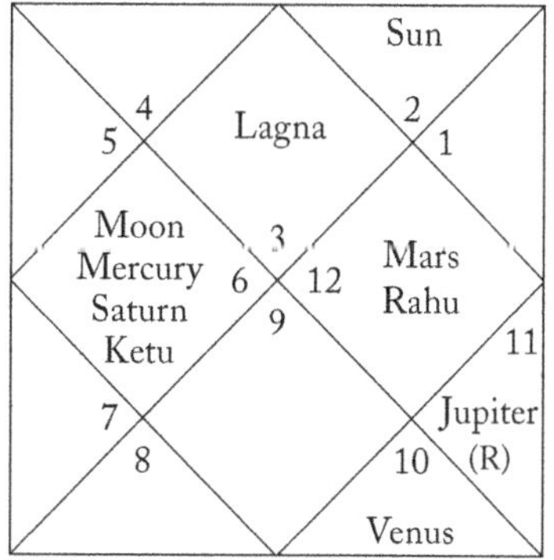

We have seen several cases where the mutual MD/AD of lagna lord and sixth lord has resulted in serious threat to health and survival. In this case, however, the eighth house is also involved along with the lagna and sixth lords. In matters where serious health issues and death are concerned, it is important to consider additional adverse factors like the sixty-fourth navamsha and the twenty-second drekkana. The reader will be well advised to look into these factors in the charts discussed here.

केवलानां च पापानां दशासु निधनं क्वचित्।
कल्पनीयं बुधैर्नृणां मारकाणामदर्शने ॥ 27 ॥

27. Sometimes (in case of non-availability of maraka dashas at the time of conclusion of longevity), the wise should consider the dashas of only (functional) malefics as relevant to the likely time of death of the natives.

Comments: As already mentioned, calculation of longevity is required for this purpose. The astrologer should then analyse the dashas and antardashas close to the likely time of death of the native. In case the dashas of the already mentioned maraka grahas are not available at that time, the wise should consider the dashas of functional malefics as indicative of the likely period of death. These include the lords of the houses 3, 6 and 11. If natural malefics own these houses and their dashas happen to operate around the time of conclusion of longevity, then such dashas can more likely cause death than the dashas of natural benefics owning these adverse houses.

मारकैः सह सम्बन्धान्निहन्ता पापकृच्छनिः।
अतिक्रम्येतरान् सर्वान् भवत्येव न संशयः॥ 28 ॥

28. A malefic Saturn, by its relationship with marakas, most certainly supersedes all others as a killer.

Comments: Amongst all the marakas, Saturn is the most potent. It is in some sense a natural maraka unless it attains special benevolence in a chart. We have seen some examples above where Saturn dasha has proved to be a maraka dasha. However, in all those examples, Saturn happened to be related to the lagna or the eighth house. It is natural for a malefic dasha involving the lagna and the eighth house to prove to be adverse. However, the verse under consideration suggests that a malefic Saturn, by associating with other marakas, supersedes them all in maraka potential. A malefic Saturn is the one which owns the third, the sixth or the eleventh (or even the eighth) house, or is ill placed. Such a Saturn, by establishing relationship with other malefics and marakas, takes over their maraka potential with some intensity.

Let us consider **chart 17** (male native, born on July 29, 1883, at 14 hours, in Predappio Alta, Italy) belonging to Benito Mussolini, the Italian dictator who ruled the country ruthlessly for over twenty years, from the year 1922 till he was deposed on July 23, 1943. Other than Rahu and Ketu, the seven grahas are confined to only three houses, viz., 8, 9 and 10. That itself creates an imbalance especially when the tenth lord Moon and the malefics Mars and Saturn occupy the eighth house without any benefic aspect. This combination is a potent raja-yoga in the eighth house with the involvement of the Moon underlining a cruel, mischievous and malicious mental makeup. The lagna lord

	Ketu	Moon Mars Saturn	Jupiter Venus
	Chart 17 (M) July 29, 1883		Sun Mercury
		Lagna Rahu	

8 Lagna Rahu 6
9 5
7
10 4 Sun Mercury
1
3
11 Ketu Jupiter Venus
12 2 Moon Mars Saturn

Lagna	28°19'	Mars	20°54'	Venus	29°19'
Sun	13°47'	Mercury	13°17'	Saturn	15°19'
Moon	16°57'	Jupiter	26°18'	Rahu	14°54'

		Jupiter Saturn	Lagna Moon Venus
Rahu	**Navamsha**		Mars
			Ketu
	Sun	Mercury	

Mars Jupiter Saturn
5 4 Lagna Moon Venus 2
Ketu 1
3
6 12
9
7 11
Mercury Rahu
8 10
Sun

Venus			Moon Saturn
Jupiter Rahu	**Dashamsha**		Lagna Sun Mars Mercury
			Ketu

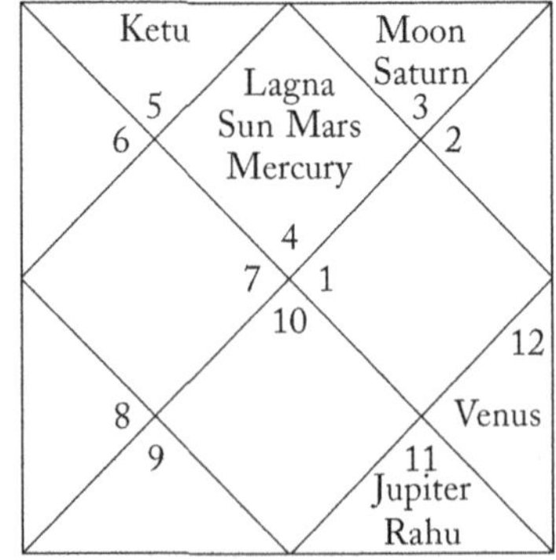

in the ninth associates with a natural benefic Jupiter which aspects the lagna, and the Sun in the tenth provides a strong administrative motivation along with an exalted tenth lord under cruel planetary influence. The dashas of Jupiter (May 1913 to May 1929) and Saturn (May 1929 till death) are important as far as his career is concerned. He was deposed on July 23, 1943 in Saturn-Rahu (December 25, 1942 to October 31, 1945) period. However, we are here concerned with his longevity and the maraka dashas.

If we roughly consider his likely lifespan, we should take into account the three groups of factors that we consider for longevity. The first group takes into consideration the lagna lord and the eighth lord. That in both cases is Venus located in a Dwiswabhava rashi, indicating *Madhyaayu*. The second group takes into account the lagna and the Moon. The lagna is a Chara rashi and the Moon a Sthira rashi. That again gives us *Madhyaayu*. When two factors give us the same lifespan, we accept that, and we do not have to go into the third group of lagna and Hora lagna. Saturn has the maraka potential despite being the yoga-karaka. It is associated with a maraka Mars which owns two maraka houses, the seventh and the second, and it is located in the adverse eighth house. The native was deposed during the Saturn-Rahu dasha, as stated above, and also executed in the same dasha (on April 28, 1945). The AD lord Rahu is located in the lagna in the sign of Venus which also is the eighth lord. So we have the MD of Saturn and the AD of the occupant of the lagna that represents the lagna lord as well as the eighth lord. The combined influence of Mars and Saturn on the eighth house, in the absence of strong mitigating factors, also sometimes tends to point to a violent, unnatural or unexpected end.

One may go into a little more detail about Saturn as qualifying for being the maraka dasha. The native qualifies for Madhyaayu for which the upper limit is 66 years and the lower limit 33 years. He was born in the dasha of Moon which dasha was followed by the dasha of Mars. Mars is a maraka but its dasha ended in 1895 when the native was only eleven years old. After that came the dasha of Rahu representing the lagna and its lord Venus. Venus is well placed and has no maraka potential. Jupiter that follows Rahu is also not a maraka. We finally come to Saturn. Saturn is a yoga-karaka but attains maraka potential by its association with a potent maraka Mars and by occupying the eighth house. The Saturn dasha with Rahu antar operates at a time which matches with our native's likely time of conclusion of longevity, and thus precipitates the event.

The *Bhavartha Ratnakara* on death-inflicting dashas

While treating matters of longevity and death, it may be of interest to the reader to know the death inflicting dashas according to another small classic, the *Bhavartha Ratnakara*. These are as follows:

1. AD of 2L in MD of 12L.
2. AD of 12L in MD of 2L.
3. 12L becomes a powerful maraka in its dasha if it is associated with or aspected by 2L.
4. Planets in the 12H which are aspected by 12L become powerful marakas during the MD of 2L.
5. Death may occur in AD of malefics occupying 12H, in the MD of 12L.
6. Malefics in 2H, if associated with 12L, cause death in their own MD/AD.
7. Death is caused by malefics in 12H, in their own MD/AD.
8. Planets associated with2L too become evil.
9. 8L in its own MD/AD may cause death.

10. Death may occur in AD of 8L within MD of 6L.
11. Malefics in 6H in their own AD's cause death.
12. Death is likely in MD of 6L and AD of occupant of 8H.
13. Planets aspected by 8L and those associated with 6L become marakas in MD of 8L.
14. Death occurs in MD of a malefic in 8H and AD of 6L.
15. Death occurs in MD of a malefic in 6H and AD of 8L.
16. Death occurs in MD of a malefic in 6H and AD of 8L in 8H.
17. Death occurs in MD of a malefic in 8H and AD of a malefic in 6H.
18. Mercury and Venus in 5H become mutual marakas.
19. Mars in 5H, if having evil lordship, kills in its own dasha.
20. Saturn in conjunction with other marakas becomes a powerful maraka (even if it is lord of favourable houses).
21. Death occurs in the dasha of 8L in the lagna.
22. If two or three sons of a native undergo Rahu dasha simultaneously, the person meets his death.

Note: We see here that most of the maraka dashas mentioned above pertain to houses 2, 6, 8 and 12.

CHAPTER 5

दशाफलाध्यायः

Chapter on Dashas

न दिशेयुर्ग्रहाः सर्वे स्वदशासु स्वभुक्तिषु ।
शुभाशुभफलं नृणामात्मभावानुरूपतः ॥ 29 ॥

29. No grahas, during their own mahadashas and their own antardashas, are likely to impart to the natives benefic or malefic results specific to their own dispositions.

Comments: A graha delivers its results to a native according to its own dispositions. The various dispositions of a graha include:

1. Lordship: A graha to a large extent grants to the native results according to the house or houses it owns in a chart.
2. Location: The placement of the graha as a house lord in a particular house, and in a particular rashi which might belong to a friend, a neutral or a foe.
3. Association with or aspect of or an exchange with another house lord modifies the results.
4. Whether the graha is a karaka or a maraka.
5. The very inherent nature of the graha itself.
6. Such additional qualifications as its strength, weakness,

combustion, retrogression, its disposition in the vargas, especially in the navamsha, etc.

Grahas tend to impart their good or adverse results to the natives during their dashas and antardashas. When there is the mahadasha of a yogakaraka graha, one tends to expect great results. However, the mahadasha of any graha is a long period and the great results do not continue all through that long duration of dasha. Saturn, for example, is a yogakaraka for Vrisha and Tula lagnas. Its mahadasha has a duration of nineteen years. We know that during the mahadasha of a graha, the antardashas of all the other grahas operate in a definite, specified order. Within the mahadasha of a graha, its own antardasha operates first of all. So, during the mahadasha of Saturn, the first antardasha would also be that of Saturn. Would yogakaraka results manifest during the MD/AD of Saturn itself? The author says 'No'. The highly beneficial yogakaraka results of a yogakaraka graha would not as a general rule manifest during its own antardasha within its own mahadasha. So also, the adverse results expected from an adverse mahadasha lord would not fructify to any large extent during its own antardasha. During the mahadasha of a graha, during its own antardasha, only general results would be expected.

आत्मसम्बन्धिनो ये च ये वा निजसधर्मिणः ।
तेषामन्तर्दशास्वेव दिशन्ति स्वदशाफलम् ॥ 30 ॥

30. They (the grahas) dispense the indicated (benefic or malefic) results of their mahadashas during the antardashas of those grahas only which are either related to them or which are of their own 'Dharma'.

Comments: The intrinsic, essential quality of a graha is its 'Dharma'. The results expected of a mahadasha lord are precipitated by the antardashas that operate within the mahadasha. A graha would not give its indicated results to the fullest during its own mahadasha and its own antardasha. It would give its indicated mahadasha results during the antardashas of those grahas which are either related to it or have an inherent nature similar to its own. Thus two factors are important in effecting the expected results from a mahadasha lord during the several antardashas that operate during its mahadasha:

1. Connectedness with the MD lord: The connection of the AD lord with the MD lord may be in any of the four forms described already, viz., conjunction, aspect, exchange, and dispositor's aspect; and
2. Similarity of nature or function with the MD lord.

Similarity of Dharma: Grahas which happen to have similar functional nature would yield similar results. They must be considered as belonging to the same Dharma. Thus kendra lords would be equivalent in function to other kendra lords, trikona lords to trikona lords, tri-shad-aaya lords to tri-shad-aaya lords, the second lord to the twelfth lord, yogakarakas to yogakarakas, and marakas to marakas. There could be a little conflict here and there. For example a trikona lord which is also the lord of an adverse house may not be exactly equivalent to another trikona lord which does not own any adverse house. Even the Dharma of a natural benefic as kendra lord would be different from that of a natural malefic as kendra lord. When there is a discrepancy, the results would be modified according to the nature and extent of the discrepancy.

It has also been suggested that pairs of houses in the horoscope could have an equivalent function and their lords could be of equivalent nature. The suggested pairs are as follows:

- Lagna lord and seventh house lord;
- Second lord and twelfth lord;
- Third lord and eleventh lord;
- Fourth lord and tenth lord;
- Fifth lord and ninth lord; and
- Sixth lord and eighth lord.

The point here is that the mahadasha lord has to yield its expected results some time during its mahadasha. Only it does not do so in its own antardasha. It yields its results during the antardashas of those grahas which are either connected with it or those which are of its own ilk, those which have a nature similar to it.

इतरेषां दशानाथविरुद्धफलदायिनाम् ।
तत्तत्फलानुगुण्येन फलान्यूह्यानि सूरिभिः ॥ 31 ॥

31. As far as the others (antardasha lords unrelated to the mahadasha lord, or of a different nature from that of the mahadasha lord), indicating contrary results to those of the mahadasha lord, are concerned, their results should be deduced by the wise according to their analytical understanding.

Comments: We have seen above, in case of antardasha lords, the importance of relationship with the mahadasha lord or of being of the same ilk as the mahadasha lord. There would be situations wherein the antardasha lord is neither related to the mahadasha lord nor of the same Dharma as the mahadasha lord. In case the nature of the antardasha lord is contrary to the nature of the mahadasha lord, the astrologer must use his wisdom, imagination and analytical understanding to arrive at the results expected of such MD/AD. In general, the AD lords which are against the nature of the MD lord will obstruct the effects of the MD lord. From what has been described till now, there could be the following situations:

- AD lord, of neutral disposition, related to the MD lord;
- AD lord, of similar disposition, related to the MD lord;
- AD lord, of contrary disposition, related to the MD lord;
- Unrelated AD lord, of neutral nature to that of the MD lord;
- Unrelated AD lord, of similar nature to that of the MD lord;
- Unrelated AD lord, of contrary nature to that of the MD lord.

The mahadasha lord is likely to manifest its expected results where the AD lord, whether neutral to, or of the nature of, the MD lord, is related to it. It will do so again where the AD lord is unrelated to it but of similar disposition to itself. In other situations where the AD lord is of contrary nature to that of the MD lord, and whether or not related to it, the astrologer must use his wisdom to arrive at any conclusion. In general, if the MD lord is a yogakaraka, the unrelated AD of a graha of contrary nature will dilute the good effects; a similar situation would exist where, in the MD of an adverse graha, the AD of a related or an unrelated yogakaraka runs.

स्वदशायां त्रिकोणेशभुक्तौ केन्द्रपतिः शुभम्।
दिशेत्सोऽपि तथा नो चेदसम्बन्धेन पापकृत् ॥ 32 ॥

32. A kendra lord in its own mahadasha, in the antardasha of a trikona lord, as also a trikona lord in its own mahadasha in the antardasha of a kendra lord, indicate benefic results (provided the two have a mutual relationship). Unrelated and blemished, their mutual dashas prove otherwise.

Comments: It has been already stated in shloka 15 earlier that strong kendra and trikona lords, even when they are blemished, yield yoga-karaka results by virtue of their mere relationship. Obviously their results would be experienced during their dashas only. For good results to follow, the mutual relationship is important. The results attributed to the mutual dashas of the kendra and the trikona lords in this shloka are 'benefic', not 'yogakaraka'. The yogakaraka results ensure high social and professional status, renown and dignity. Obviously, yogakaraka results, or highly special benefic results, will only be there when the condition mentioned in shloka '14' is fulfilled. That is, when the trikona and kendra lords under consideration are totally unblemished. Their results would not be benefic if they are not related mutually. Further, the results would be adverse if they are blemished on the one hand and not related to the mahadasha lord on the other. In this classic there is so much stress on mutual relationship or mutual connectedness. The best and most complete results of a given mahadasha are experienced only during the antardasha of a graha which has a mutual connectedness with the mahadasha lord. If this mutual connectedness is missing, the antardasha lord has to be of the same ilk as the mahadasha lord for the results of the mahadasha lord to be experienced.

The results of the mutual MD/AD of kendra and trikona lords may be broadly categorised as follows:

A. When MD and AD lords are mutually related:

1. Unblemished natural malefic as kendra lord and unblemished trikona lord: Excellent results;
2. Blemished natural malefic as kendra lord and unblemished trikona lord: Very good results;
3. Unblemished natural benefic as kendra lord and unblemished trikona lord: Very good results;
4. Blemished natural benefic as kendra lord and unblemished trikona lord: Very good results;
5. Unblemished natural malefic as kendra lord and blemished trikona lord: Good results;
6. Blemished natural malefic as kendra lord and blemished trikona lord: Good results;
7. Unblemished natural benefic as kendra lord and blemished trikona lord: Good to average results;
8. Blemished natural benefic as kendra lord and blemished trikona lord: Average results.

B. When MD and AD lords are not mutually related:

1. Both unblemished: Average results;
2. Both blemished: Very adverse results;
3. One blemished and the other unblemished: Adverse results.

It is thus obvious that being related with each other is an important quality for the MD and AD lords. A mutual relationship enhances and ensures the results that the MD lord (as well as the AD lord) would be expected to deliver.

आरम्भो राजयोगस्य भवेन्मारकभुक्तिषु ।
प्रथयन्ति तमारभ्य क्रमशः पापभुक्तयः ॥ 33 ॥

तत्सम्बन्धिशुभानां च तथा पुनरसंयुजाम् ।
शुभानां तु समत्वेन संयोगो योगकारिणाम् ॥ 34 ॥

33, 34. (In the mahadasha of a yogakaraka), a raja-yoga that commences in the antardashas of marakas gets further enforcement in the antardashas of those malefics which are related to the mahadasha lord. Antardashas of related benefics yield similar good results.

Antardashas of unrelated benefics give only ordinary results while those of unrelated yoga-karakas give good results.

Comments: When the dasha of a yogakaraka graha is in operation, good results are naturally expected. If during the dasha of a yogakaraka graha, there is a maraka antardasha in operation and a rajayoga precipitates during that dasha, the subsequent malefic antardashas continue to support that rajayoga. This is especially so if the malefic antardasha lords are related to the mahadasha lord. Antardashas of related benefics provide similar support. Antardashas of unrelated benefics too do not give very bad results; instead they give average results only. Unrelated yogakarakas give some good results.

The reader is referred to **chart 18** (Bill Clinton, born on August 19, 1946, at 8:51 hours, at Hope, Arkansas, USA). This charismatic former US President has an interesting horoscope. The lagna is Kanya with the lagna lord (as

	Moon	Rahu	
	Chart 18 (M) August 19, 1946		Mercury Saturn
			Sun
	Ketu	Jupiter	Lagna Mars Venus

Jupiter Sun
8 4
7 Lagna Mars Venus 5
Ketu Mer Saturn
6
9 3
12
2
10 Rahu
11 1
Moon

Lagna	12°23'	Mars	13°14'	Venus	18°00'
Sun	02°53'	Mercury	14°30'	Saturn	09°01'
Moon	27°11'	Jupiter	00°06'	Rahu	25°09'

	Lagna Sun Mars		Venus
Ketu	**Navamsha**		
			Rahu
Moon	Mercury	Jupiter	Saturn

3 11
2 Lagna Sun Mars 12
Venus Ketu
1
4 10
7
5 9
Rahu Jupiter Moon
6 8
Saturn Mercury

Ketu			Saturn
	Dashamsha		Mercury
Moon			Sun
	Venus	Jupiter	Lagna Mars Rahu

Jupiter Sun
8 4
7 Lagna Mars Rahu 5
Venus Mercury
6
9 3 Saturn
12
10
Moon Ketu 2
11 1

well as the tenth lord) Mercury forming a strong raja-yoga by associating with the fifth (and sixth) lord Saturn in the eleventh house. The lagna is occupied by the benefic ninth lord which gets debilitated in the lagna, and further associates with the malefic eighth lord Mars. The ninth lord gets blemished by debilitation, eighth lord association and also the aspect of the sixth (and fifth) lord Saturn. A vargottama Jupiter in the second house forms a Gajakesari yoga by being located in the seventh house from the Moon which, according to our understanding of its eleventh lordship, is a malefic. The Moon further receives aspects of Mars, Saturn and Jupiter. Rahu in the ninth house is exalted (Vrisha is considered the exaltation sign of Rahu) and its dispositor Venus is debilitated and afflicted in the lagna. An afflicted Moon in the eighth house is an adverse yoga causing Balarishta, indicating suffering in childhood, whether physical or mental. His father died three months before his birth and he was raised by an alcoholic stepfather.

An exalted Sun along with the navamsha lagna lord Mars occupies the navamsha lagna, and a vargottama Jupiter from the seventh house aspects this combination in the lagna, and also Ketu and Venus in the eleventh and the third houses respectively. The dashamsha chart too shows a strong Sun in its own house. Jupiter, Mars, Mercury, Saturn, Moon, Rahu and Ketu all remain significant for his Karma or profession as they either own or aspect or occupy houses significant for profession in the dashamsha chart. Only Venus remains a little aloof though its dipositor Mars occupies the lagna of the dashamsha chart and thus remains relevant to his professional work. This indicates a man of multiple interests. A strong Sun also ensures name and fame for the native, whether in or out of office, despite several controversies and sexual misdemeanours thanks to a weak and afflicted Venus.

The native gained significant social status when he became the Governor of the state of Arkansas for the first time from January 9, 1979 to January 19, 1981. The operative dashas during that period were Rahu-Mercury (May 5, 1977 to November 22, 1979), Rahu-Ketu (November 22, 1979 to December 10, 1980) and Rahu-Venus (December 10, 1980 to December 11, 1983). He lost the next election but came back subsequently and remained the Governor of Arkansas for four successive terms, from January 11, 1983 to December 12, 1992 when he resigned. The operative dashas during this period were Rahu-Venus, Rahu-Sun, Rahu-Moon, Rahu-Mars, Jupiter-Jupiter, Jupiter-Saturn and Jupiter-Mercury (from December 10, 1980 to April 29, 1992). The return to Governorship in Rahu-Venus also points to another principle of astrology mentioned in the shloka under consideration. According to this, a raja-yoga which commences in the antardasha of a maraka gets further enhancement during the subsequent antardashas. Venus here is also the second lord and a maraka. The raja-yoga that commenced in Rahu-Venus continued into subsequent antardashas too. Even Jupiter is a maraka and its antardasha only continued with the raja-yoga that had commenced already. It needs to be taken note of that Jupiter is the lord of the seventh house, and Venus the karaka for the seventh house is debilitated and grossly afflicted. The several AD's during the MD of Jupiter brought to the fore the numerous sexual misadventures that the native indulged in rather indiscriminately. These haunted him even when he enjoyed the potent raja-yogas.

We notice that the good period starts from Rahu-Mercury dasha. Rahu is exalted in a trikona and, true to its nature, it behaves as an exalted trikona lord. The AD of the lagna lord and tenth lord Mercury during the MD of an exalted trikona lord has to give excellent results during its dasha. While Ketu, the next AD lord, is a malefic, the subsequent AD is that of the ninth lord Venus. So, between two benefic dashas, the intervening malefic dasha of Ketu only continues to give good results (see comments to shlokas 18 and 19 made earlier). While he loses in the next term elections, he comes back after two years, toward the later part of the Rahu-Venus dasha itself. Another sound principle of Vedic astrology operates here. Venus, the AD lord, is debilitated and afflicted, hence it is weak. However, it gets rejuvenation because of Neecha-Bhanga (cancellation of debilitation) raja-yoga. This Neecha-Bhanga of Venus is effected by its exaltation lord Jupiter and its debilitation lord Mercury being located in mutual kendras from each other and from the Moon. A planet with Neecha-Bhanga gives adverse results during the early part of its dasha but resumes its good effect after some time. One must see the dasha order that the native got from Rahu-Mercury onwards. We have already explained Ketu and Venus. Then comes the AD of the Sun in its own house in the rashi and dashamsha charts and exalted in the navamsha; the Moon, participant in the Gajakesari yoga; and finally Mars, occupying the lagna in the navamsha and dashamsha charts as well, besides in the rashi chart. Here comes another principle of Parashara. When the same graha occupies or aspects the lagna in the shadvargas (the six varga charts, viz., rashi, hora, drekkana, navamsha, dwadashamsha and trimshamsha), it produces a raja-yoga. Mars does that except in the dwadashamsha chart!

Rahu dasha ends on May 24, 1987 and Jupiter dasha commences. Jupiter's AD during its own MD operates from May 24, 1987 to July 11, 1989. The yoga effects of Jupiter manifest more intensely when the AD of Saturn starts. Jupiter-Saturn is the MD-AD of a kendra lord and a trikona lord. His Governorship continues into Jupiter-Mercury dasha when he resigned to assume the office of President of the United States. He was sworn into office as US President on January 20, 1993 during Jupiter-Mercury (January 22, 1992 to April 29, 1994). While Jupiter suffers the blemish of kendra lordship, the seventh house lordship is also meant for enhancement of status ('Padonnati') according to sage Parashara. Jupiter is vargottama and forms a powerful Gaja-Kesari yoga. We are mainly concerned with the order of AD's here. The AD lord Mercury is a strong benefic because of its lagna lordship, besides the lordship of the strongest kendra, the tenth house. It is associated with a trikona lord Saturn (which has some blemish of the sixth lordship too). The two are situated in the tenth house from the dasha lord Jupiter. The native got a strong raja-yoga effect despite some blemishes of Jupiter and Saturn.

The next dasha is that of Jupiter-Ketu, from April 29, 1994 to April 5, 1995. Ketu is a natural malefic and its dispositor, whom Ketu represents, i.e., Mars, is a strong functional malefic for Kanya lagna. After this AD comes the next AD of Venus (April 5, 1995 to December 4, 1997). Venus is the lord of the ninth house, a trikona, and a functional benefic for Kanya lagna. Other than its association with the malefic Mars, it is aspected by the trikona lord Saturn. The malefic AD of Ketu intervening between two benefic dashas only gave desirable results, like it did during the Rahu-Ketu dasha earlier, and the raja-yoga continued without interruption. During the Venus AD, the native was re-elected to the high office and sworn in as the US President for the second time on January 20, 1997. However, during this very AD, and extending into the next one which was the AD of the Sun (December 4, 1997 to September 22, 1998), controversies arose about his sexual misconduct with a White House intern. There was already no dearth of incidents of sexual misdemeanours but this one turned rather serious. It must be noted that Venus is debilitated, associated with a malefic Mars which is the eighth lord of scandals, and aspected by the sixth lord Saturn. Venus remains under the aspect of Saturn in the navamsha chart as well. Thus good effects of rajayogas exist along with adverse effects indicated by the adverse lordship and associations of yoga-forming grahas.

The next two AD's (Moon and Mars) last till December 28, 2000, close to the end of his term of Presidency. The AD of Moon (September 22, 1998 to January 22, 2000) saw him suffer the humiliation of impeachment proceedings against him. It was on December 19, 1998 that motion was passed to adopt impeachment proceedings against him. He was, however, ultimately acquitted on February 12, 1999 as the Senate did not reach the two-thirds majority vote required in spite of the ferocious campaign against him. On his last day in office, he surrendered his license to practice law for five years in exchange for the end of investigation and an agreement that the grand jury not seek an indictment. The military strike that the native ordered against Iraq on December 16, 1998 was alleged to be aimed to distract attention from his trial. The President, however, maintained that the strike was ordered because of noncooperation of the regime of Saddam Hussein with the UN weapons examiners. The Moon in the eighth house of scandals is aspected by the seventh lord Jupiter, sixth lord Saturn and eighth lord Mars, all pointing to sexual scandals and a vicious and malicious campaign against the native.

It may be noted that the native had the last AD of Rahu in the MD of Jupiter ending on May 23, 2003. After that commenced the MD of Saturn. The native has been extremely active in his Saturn MD. He has been lecturing extensively, using his oratorical skills to great use. According to an estimate, the overall earnings of the native from his 542 paid speeches between January 2001 and January 2013 have been more than US $ 104 million. He has also resorted to writing books which have been bestsellers, and has been undertaking philanthropic work after his Presidency.

The dasha has created some health issues for the native for which he has taken appropriate treatment. Saturn, the MD lord, is the lord of the fifth house, a trikona, and also of the sixth house (disease). Its association with the lagna lord, though forming a raja-yoga, is not too good for health. The second house, with the benefic Jupiter in it, is the house for speech while the fifth is the house for eloquence. According to the *Bhavartha Ratnakara*, a native born in Kanya lagna experiences 'yoga' result during the Saturn dasha provided this Saturn is located in the eleventh house. The presence of a strong raja-yoga in the eleventh house also points out to the massive earnings that the native has experienced soon after the commencement of the Saturn dasha.

शुभस्यास्य प्रसक्तस्य दशायां योगकारकाः ।
स्वभुक्तिषु प्रयच्छन्ति कुत्रचिद्योगजं फलम् ॥ 35 ॥

35. During the mahadasha of a benefic, its related yogakarakas in their antardashas occasionally give raja yoga.

Comments: Earlier we have discussed the various antardashas operating during the mahadashas of yogakarakas. Here is a situation where the mahadasha is supposed to be that of a benefic graha and the antardasha of a yogakaraka. The text states that on occasion during the mahadasha of a benefic graha, the antardasha of a related yogakaraka graha is also likely to give results like those of a yogakaraka. The point is that the mahadasha lord decides on the overall nature of results that would ensue during the antardashas that operate within its mahadasha. Thus, the mahadasha lord that is only benefic and not a yogakaraka can only give benefic results. The yogakaraka during its antardasha would only be able to give good results to the extent the mahadasha lord permits. Hence, it can only occasionally give yoga results.

There is another version of the shloka. We have used the word 'prasaktasya' (प्रसक्तस्य) meaning 'of the one related' instead of the alternate 'viyuktasya' (वियुक्तस्य) meaning 'of the one unrelated'. In case we take the alternate version, the shloka would read: 'During the mahadasha of a benefic, the antardashas of its unrelated yogakarakas occasionally give raja yoga.' This would mean that during the mahadasha of a benefic, the yogakarakas that are related to it would certainly give yoga results. However, even the unrelated yogakarakas during their antardashas on occasion give good results.

तमोग्रहौ शुभारूढावसम्बन्धेन केनचित्।
अन्तर्दशानुसारेण भवेतां योगकारकौ ॥ 36 ॥

36. Rahu and Ketu, in auspicious houses (kendras and trikonas), unrelated with others, give yoga-karaka results according to (the nature of) the antardasha.

Comments: We have already noted in chart 18 above how Rahu in his ninth house gave good results to the native. Rahu as an exalted shadowy planet behaves as an exalted lord of the house it occupies. Besides, it gives results according to the nature of the AD lords. This Rahu is neither associated with another graha nor aspected by any one. Hence it can give its results freely and without any modification. Rahu in the above case started giving particularly good results once the AD of the lagna lord and tenth lord Mercury started, from May 1977 onwards.

Let us consider the chart of another past President of the USA whose Rahu dasha proved to be a yoga-karaka dasha for him and who remains in the memory of the USA several years after his death. **Chart 19** belonging to John F. Kennedy (born on May 29, 1917, at 15:01 hours in Brookline, Massachusetts, USA) shows Kanya lagna with the lagna lord (and tenth lord) Mercury in the adverse eighth house, associated with the eighth lord Mars and aspected by the sixth (and fifth) lord Saturn. His Rahu is situated in the fourth house in a sign of Jupiter, alone, with no association or aspect. So it is capable of giving yogakaraka results according to the antardashas that would operate during its mahadasha. The mahadasha of Rahu operated from August 24, 1943 to August 23, 1961. At the commencement of the Rahu dasha, Kennedy was already serving in the American Navy. He had survived arduous situations at sea toward the end of his earlier dasha of Mars, the eighth lord afflicted in the eighth house. Rahu-Rahu dasha was a change for the better. He got military decorations and awards (including Purple Heart in 1945) for his extremely heroic conduct, his outstanding courage and his leadership qualities soon after he entered the Rahu dasha.

The native entered politics and was elected to the US House of Representatives on November 5, 1946. This was Rahu-Jupiter dasha (May 6, 1946 to September 28, 1948). Rahu remains significant in the navamsha and dashamsha charts occupying the lagna in the one and the fifth house in the other. Jupiter as a kendra lord associates with the ninth lord Venus and the royal Sun in the ninth house. He was re-elected in November 1948 and November 1950 during Rahu-Saturn, the MD of a Rahu in a kendra and the AD of a trikona lord. In November 1952, he was elected to the US Senate during the dasha of Rahu-Mercury (August 5, 1951 to February 22, 1954). The AD lord Mercury is the

	Mars Mercury	Sun Jupiter Venus	Ketu
	Chart 19 May 29, 1917		Saturn
			Moon
Rahu			Lagna

Moon 4
7 8 Lagna 5 Saturn
Rahu 9 6 3 12 Ketu
2 Sun Jupiter Venus
10 11 1 Mars Mercury

Lagna	27°28'	Mars	25°43'	Venus	24°02'
Sun	15°08'	Mercury	27°53'	Saturn	04°27'
Moon	24°30'	Jupiter	00°20'	Rahu	18°32'

Ketu		Sun	
	Navamsha		
Jupiter			Venus Saturn
Mercury	Moon Mars		Lagna Rahu

8 Moon Mars 7
Lagna Rahu
Venus Saturn 5 4
Mercury 9 6 3 12
10 Jupiter 11
Ketu
2 Sun 1

	Moon Saturn		Sun Rahu
Lagna	**Dashamsha**		
Mercury Jupiter			
Mars Ketu			Venus

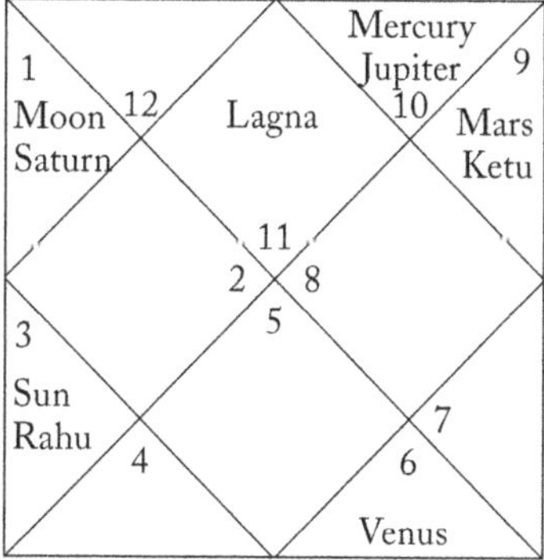

	Moon Rahu	Lagna Jupiter	
	Drekkana		Saturn
Venus			
Mars Mercury		Ketu	Sun

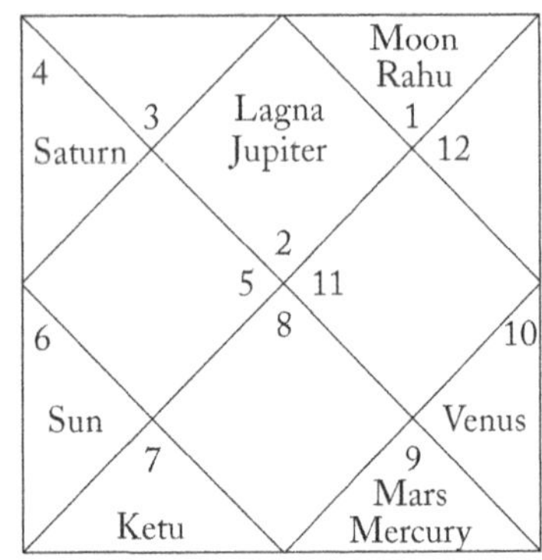

lord of the lagna and of the strongest kendra, the tenth house.

By 1956, JFK enjoyed name and recognition, politically and as an author. At the August 1956 Democratic Convention in Chicago, during his Rahu-Venus dasha (March 12, 1955 to March 12, 1958), he made a run for the Vice Presidential nomination. While his bid for the Democratic Vice Presidential nomination failed, he gained the respect of the Democratic delegates and national prominence, but was not saddled with a spot on Adlai Stevenson's losing ticket. Venus has the blemish of being debilitated in the dashamsha where it is also located in the adverse eighth house, but also enjoys an effective Neecha-Bhanga because of the conjunction of its debilitation and exaltation lords, Mercury and Jupiter. A neecha graha with a Neecha-Bhanga gives an initial jolt but eventually ensures recovery. During this very dasha, his work 'Profiles in Courage' was awarded the Pulitzer Prize. The native won re-election to the Senate on November 4, 1958 during the Rahu-Sun dasha (March 12, 1958 to February 4, 1959). The Sun is associated with yogakaraka grahas in the rashi chart, is vargottama, and associates as a kendra lord with Rahu in a trikona in the dashamsha.

It was on January 2, 1960 that Kennedy announced his candidacy for the Democratic Presidential Nomination. The dasha was Rahu-Moon (February 4, 1959 to August 4, 1960). The Moon is the eleventh lord and not to be considered a benefic. In the navamsha, the Moon is debilitated with a cancellation and in the dashamsha it is an adverse lord though associated with the lagna lord. There were opponents to his candidacy but his personal charisma, his eloquence and his money earned him supporters. Uncertainties remained during the election campaign. Considered from Rahu in Dhanu, the Moon is the eighth lord in the ninth house and not a malefic. He won the election on November 8, 1960 and took office on January 20, 1961. The operating dasha at that time was Rahu-Mars (August 4, 1960 to August 23, 1961). Mars is a strong graha in the rashi, the navamsha and dashamsha charts and derives strength from the lagna and tenth lord Mercury and the fifth lord Saturn in the rashi chart. But while Mars derives strength, it in return afflicts these same grahas.

The native was a strong proponent of peace and human rights, an opponent of the death penalty and an advocate of racial integration. He administered several reforms which were long overdue. The benefic combination of grahas in the ninth house signifies the benevolence in his nature. Kennedy soon became a popular world leader. It was at the height of his popularity that he was struck by an assassin's bullet on November 22, 1963 and died. The dasha operating at the time of his death was that of Jupiter-Saturn (October 11, 1963 to April 23, 1966). Jupiter is the seventh lord, a maraka, while Saturn is the sixth lord aspected by the eighth lord Mars. Jupiter gets additional maraka potential by being the lord of the twenty-second drekkana while Saturn gets aspected by Mars from the twenty-second drekkana (eighth house of the drekkana chart). The raja-yoga that started in the antardasha of the eighth lord, potentially a death inflictor, ended in the death of the native during the next maraka dasha influenced by the same eighth lord.

Another important aspect of this chart is that it prominently indicates poor health for the native. The lagna lord occupies the adverse eighth house, associated with the eighth lord, and aspected by the sixth lord. The adverse grahas are Mars and Saturn. The native had longstanding health issues. He had multiple operations on his back. He suffered infections of the urinary tract for decades and had chronic stomach problems. He also suffered from Addison's disease, a deficiency of adrenal function, with consequently poor immune system. An afflicted Venus in the navamsha and the drekkana indicates intervertebral disc problems, urinary ailments and hormone deficiencies. Despite all this, his courage, intelligence and good looks stood him in good stead and he always remained a popular figure.

CHAPTER 6

मिश्रफलाध्यायः
The Miscellany

पापा यदि दशानाथाः शुभानां तदसंयुजाम्।
भुक्तयः पापफलदास्तत्संयुक्शुभभुक्तयः ॥ 37 ॥

भवन्ति मिश्रफलदा भुक्तयो योगकारिणाम्।
अत्यन्तपापफलदा भवन्ति तदसंयुजाम् ॥ 38 ॥

37, 38. During the mahadashas of malefics, the antardashas of unrelated benefics give malefic results; antardashas of related benefics give mixed results; antardashas of related yogakarakas also give mixed results, while those of unrelated yogakarakas give extremely malefic results.

Comments: Whenever there is a mention of benefics and malefics in this text, whether here or elsewhere, only the functional benefics and functional malefics are meant. One expects adverse results during the dashas of malefics. However, the results of the dashas of malefics also get modified during the various antardashas. How adverse they would prove to be depends on whether the antardasha lords are related with the mahadasha lords or not. The importance of connectedness, or being related with, has been highlighted in this text at several places. Here too, the results of various antardashas during the mahadasha of a malefic have been mentioned depending upon their being or not being related to, or connected with, the mahadasha lord. The following points have been stressed upon in the shloka under consideration:

1. During the mahadashas of malefics, the antardashas of benfics not connected with them give adverse results;
2. During the mahadashas of malefics, the antardashas of benefics connected with them give mixed results;
3. During the mahadashas of malefics, the antardashas of yogakarakas connected with them give mixed results;
4. During the mahadashas of malefics, the antardashas of yogakarakas not connected with them give extremely malefic results.

The connection of one graha with another has to be in one of the four ways described already. By connecting with the mahadasha lord, the benefic antardasha lord gets some scope to give its benefic result. Hence the native enjoys mixed results during such a dasha. When the antardasha lord is not related with the mahadasha lord, the antardasha lord does not find expression. If it is a benefic antardasha lord, the results are malefic. If it is a yogakaraka antardasha lord, the results, according to this classic, are excessively malefic. Needless to say, if there is the mahadasha of a malefic in operation and the antardasha of another malefic graha either related or unrelated to the mahadasha lord, the results will be adverse (see **chart 6**).

We have earlier seen that during the mahadashas of yogakarakas, the related malefics also give good results during their antardashas. Thus the malefic antardasha lords tend to change for the better by associating with a benefic mahadasha lord. In the shloka under consideration, it is conveyed that during the mahadasha of a malefic, the antardasha of a related benefic tends to give mixed results, i.e., neither too good nor too bad results. Here it appears as if the mahadasha lord is to some extent being modified for the better by its association with a benefic antardasha lord.

सत्यपि स्वेन सम्बन्धे न हन्ति शुभभुक्तिषु ।
हन्ति सत्यप्यसम्बन्धे मारकः पापभुक्तिषु ॥ 39 ॥

39. A maraka does not prove to be a killer during its mahadasha in the antardasha of its related benefic. It, however, kills during the antardasha of an unrelated malefic.

Comments: We have seen in **chart 19** above that the native died in the dasha of Jupiter-Saturn. Jupiter is the maraka, being the lord of the seventh house. Saturn is a malefic by lordship and unrelated to the mahadasha lord. The reader is also referred to shloka 28 above where it is stated that a malefic Saturn by its relationship with marakas supersedes all others as a killer. In the chart under consideration, Saturn is a malefic sixth lord. It has no relationship with another maraka but is aspected by the most malefic eighth lord Mars from the eighth house. Its antardasha under the mahadasha of a maraka Jupiter proved fatal.

परस्परदशायां स्वभुक्तौ सूर्यजभार्गवौ ।
व्यत्ययेन विशेषेण प्रदिशेतां शुभाशुभम् ॥ 40 ॥

40. In their mutual mahadashas and antardashas, Saturn and Venus specially exchange good or evil results of each other.

Comments: Mutual dashas and antardashas of Venus and Saturn hold special place for astrologers. We know that the mahadasha lord expresses itself through the antardashas that operate within its operational period. It expresses itself through the antardashas of the grahas which are either connected with it or belong to its own Dharma. In the shloka under consideration, our author does not mention the need for the grahas to be connected with each other or to belong to the same Dharma in the case of the mutual dasha-antardasha of Saturn and Venus. While this seems to be an exception, the reason is not far to seek. Saturn and Venus hold a special mutual relationship in astrology. We know that for the lagnas of Venus (Vrisha and Tula), Saturn is a yogakaraka, being a kendra and a trikona lord for both lagnas. Similarly, for the lagnas of Saturn (Makara and Kumbha), Venus happens to be the yogakaraka, being a kendra and a trikona lord for both lagnas.

While several authors have attributed special results to mutual dasha-antardasha of Saturn and Venus, we shall come to those opinions later. Let us first examine, according to the concepts of our present author, the charts of three US politicians who all ran the Saturn-Venus dasha during the 2016 presidential elections.

Chart 20 (male native, born on November 23, 1950, at 11 hours, in Brooklyn, New York, USA) belongs to US senator Charles Schumer of the Democratic Party. He was running Saturn-Venus (July 2, 2014 to September 1, 2017) during the 2016 US elections. He won comfortably, joined office on January 3, 2017 and was unanimously elected the Minority Leader of the Democratic Party. According to our author, Venus as the antardasha lord should give results of Saturn. On its own, the yogakaraka Venus would be expected to give good results during its dasha. Some trouble could be expected though because of its being afflicted by

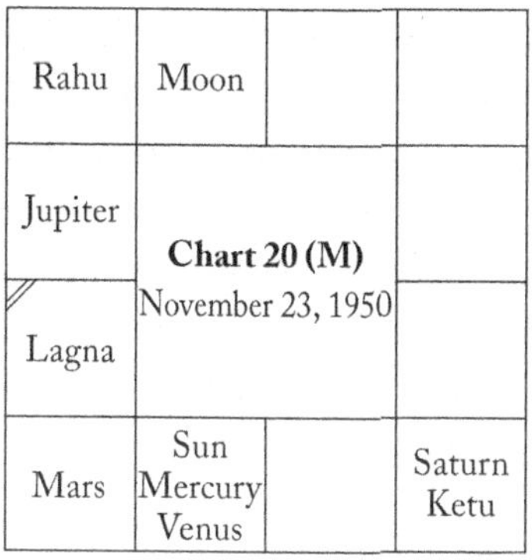

Rahu	Moon		
Jupiter	**Chart 20 (M)** November 23, 1950		
Lagna			
Mars	Sun Mercury Venus		Saturn Ketu

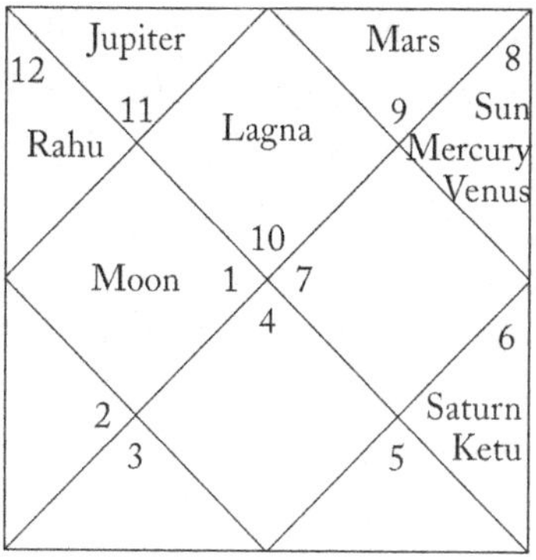

Jupiter
12
11
Rahu
Lagna
Mars
8
9
Sun Mercury Venus
Moon
10
1
7
4
6
Saturn Ketu
2
3
5

Lagna	03°53'	Mars	20°01'	Venus	10°01'
Sun	07°37'	Mercury	19°54'	Saturn	07°04'
Moon	27°06'	Jupiter	05°56'	Rahu	03°09'

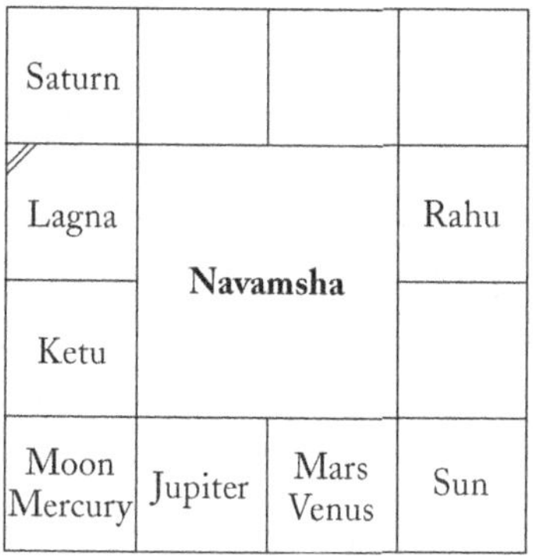

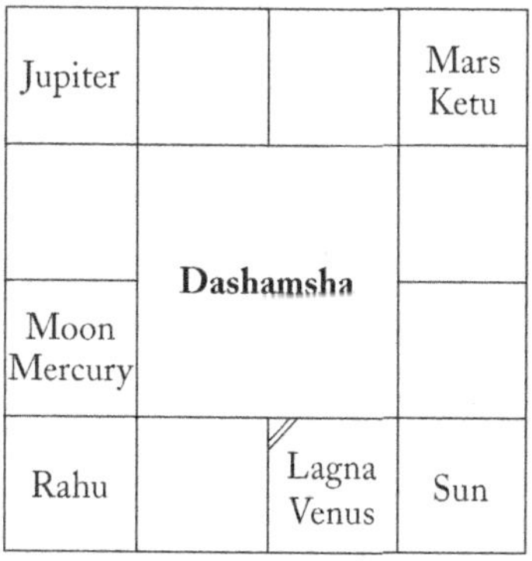

Saturn			
Lagna	**Navamsha**		Rahu
Ketu			
Moon Mercury	Jupiter	Mars Venus	Sun

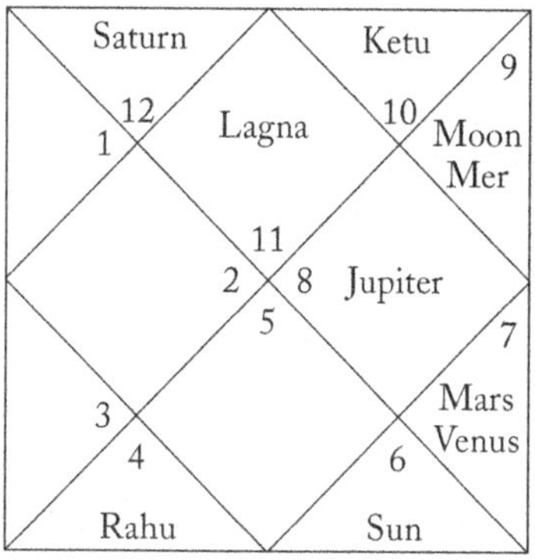

Saturn
12
1
Lagna
Ketu
9
10
Moon Mer
11
2
8
Jupiter
5
7
Mars Venus
3
4
Rahu
6
Sun

Jupiter			Mars Ketu
	Dashamsha		
Moon Mercury			
Rahu		Lagna Venus	Sun

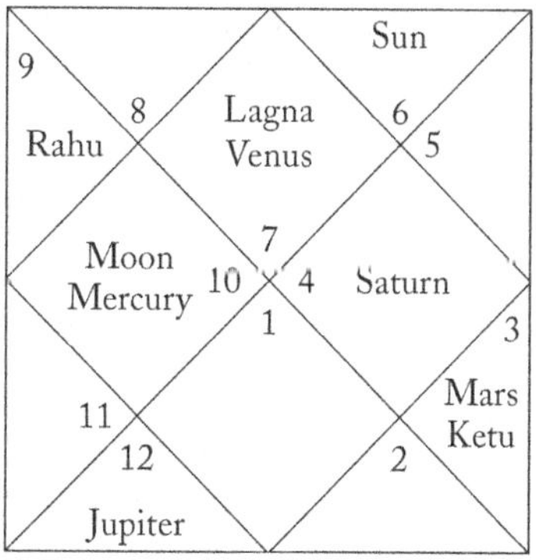

9
Rahu
8
Lagna Venus
Sun
6
5
Moon Mercury
7
10
4
Saturn
1
3
Mars Ketu
11
12
Jupiter
2

the sixth and the eighth lords. However, the favourable results become certain when it represents the lagna lord Saturn. Saturn as the lagna lord associates with Ketu in the ninth house forming a potent rajayoga. Saturn and Venus remain significant in the navamsha and dashamsha charts too. In the navamsha, Saturn is the lagna lord while the yogakaraka Venus forms a rajayoga in the ninth house in association with the tenth lord Mars. In the dashamsha, Venus occupies the Tula lagna and Saturn, the yogakaraka, occupies the tenth house aspected by the ninth and tenth lords, the Moon and Mercury.

We next take up the chart of Paul Ryan (**chart 21**, born on January 29, 1970 at 2:37 hours, in Janesville, Wisconsin, USA) who ran his Saturn-Venus dasha from December 28, 2013 to February 27, 2017. The native has Vrishchika lagna. Coming from the Republican Party, he was elected Speaker of the House of Representatives on October 29, 2015 after his predecessor resigned. Then again, two months after the 2016 presidential elections, the native was re-elected Speaker of the House on January 3, 2017. During both these terms, he was running the Saturn-Venus dasha. Saturn is the debilitated fourth (and third) lord located in the sixth house and aspected by the yogakarakas Moon and Jupiter from the twelfth house. Another unusual yoga forms with two kendra lords, Sun and Venus, in the third house owned by Saturn, aspected by their dispositor Saturn. In the navamsha, the Saturn-Venus conjunction in the tenth house is a potent rajayoga, being a combination of two trikona lords in a kendra. In the dashamsha again, Saturn participates in a rajayoga by being the fifth lord and conjoining with the tenth and the lagna lord Mercury. Venus has to deliver the results of this Saturn only. He did not go for the next elections which were to be held in November 2018 and demitted office on January 3, 2019 during Saturn-Moon (February 9, 2018 to September 2019). The Moon is an

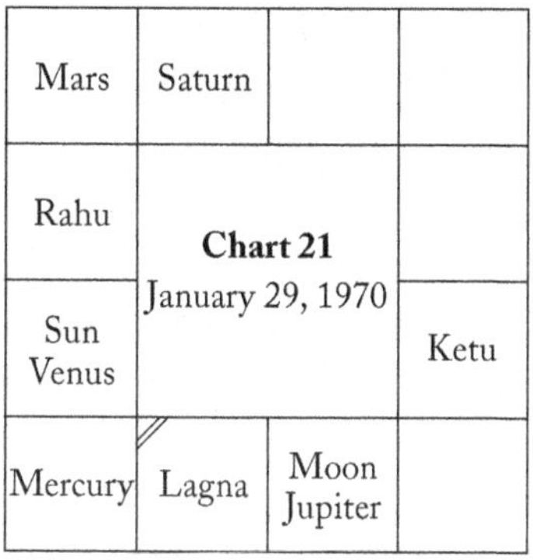

Mars	Saturn		
Rahu	**Chart 21** January 29, 1970		
Sun Venus			Ketu
Mercury	Lagna	Moon Jupiter	

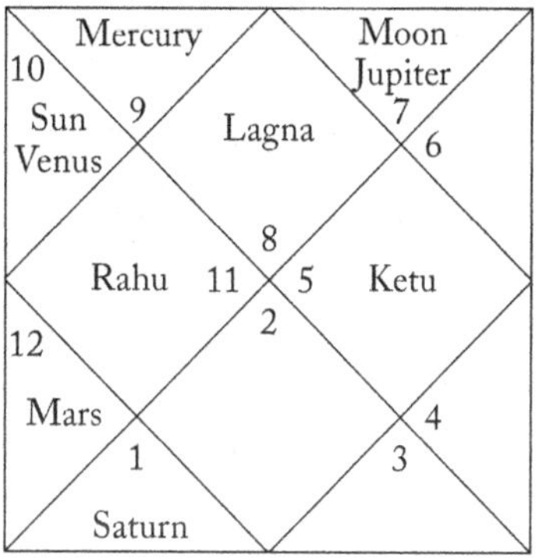

Mercury
10
9
Sun
Venus
Lagna
Moon
Jupiter
7
6
8
Rahu 11
5 Ketu
2
12
Mars
1
4
3
Saturn

Lagna	07°11'	Mars	09°51'	Venus	16°40'
Sun	15°35'	Mercury	21°43'	Saturn	09°12'
Moon	00°45'	Jupiter	11°48'	Rahu	18°47'

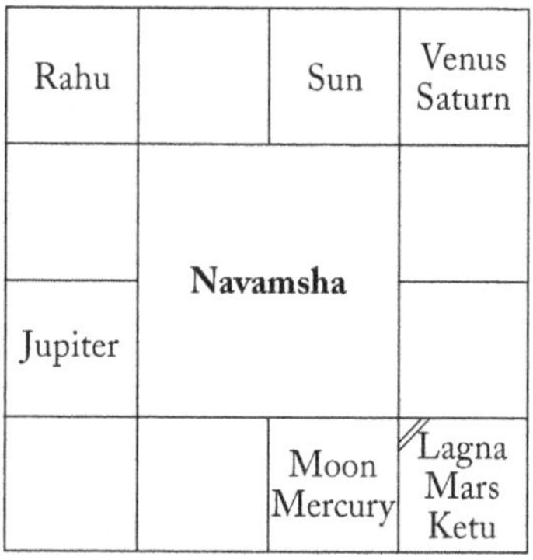

Rahu		Sun	Venus Saturn
	Navamsha		
Jupiter			
		Moon Mercury	Lagna Mars Ketu

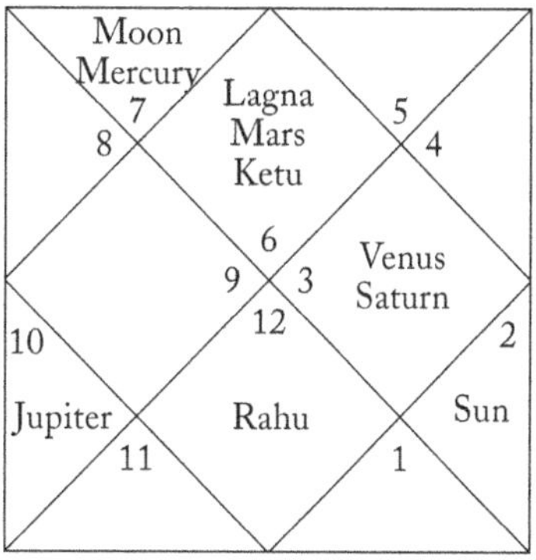

Moon
Mercury
7
8
Lagna
Mars
Ketu
5
4
6
9
3
Venus
Saturn
12
10
2
Jupiter
Rahu
Sun
11
1

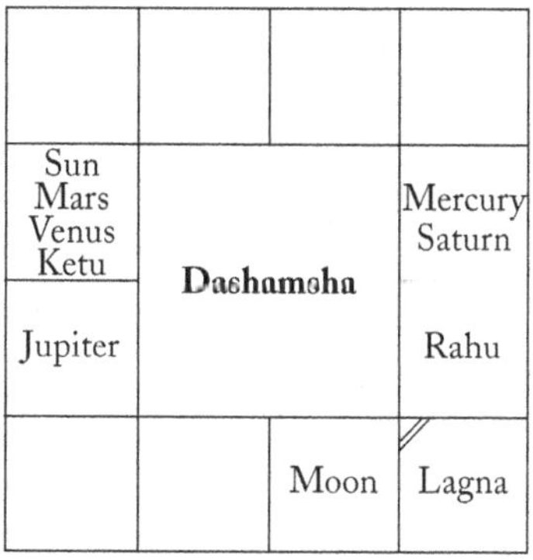

Sun Mars Venus Ketu	**Dashamsha**		Mercury Saturn
Jupiter			Rahu
		Moon	Lagna

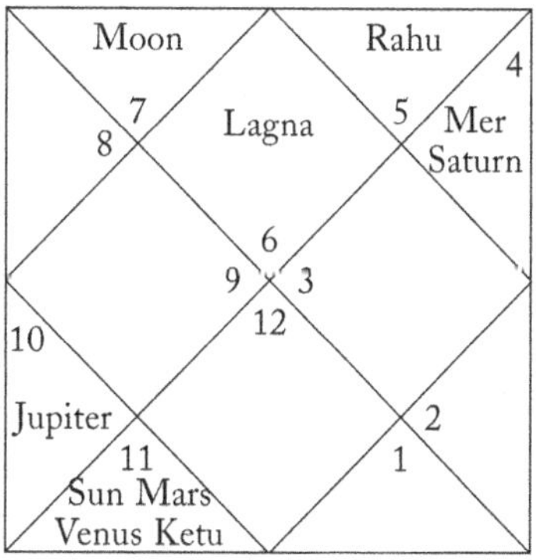

Moon
Rahu
4
7
8
Lagna
5
Mer
Saturn
6
9
3
12
10
Jupiter
2
11
1
Sun Mars
Venus Ketu

adverse house lord in both the navamsha and the dashamsha.

According to another classic, which we shall soon refer to, the debilitation of Saturn in the rashi chart can also be taken as a positive factor as far as the Saturn-Venus dasha results are concerned.

Another US senator who fought the elections in November 2016 as Vice Presidential running mate to Hillary Clinton, and lost, was Tim Kaine (**chart 22**, born on February 26, 1958, at 7:59 hours, in Saint Paul, Minnesota, USA). He was running his Saturn-Venus dasha from April 13, 2015 to June 12, 2018. For Meena lagna, both Saturn and Venus own adverse houses. Their mutual dasha-antardasha would ordinarily also not be likely to yield any great results. In any case, Venus here would be expected to give the results that are to be expected from Saturn. Saturn owns the most malefic eleventh house, along with the twelfth, and Venus is the malefic third and eighth lord. Saturn gets debilitated in the navamsha and associates with the tenth lord Moon while Venus gets exalted. Venus, however, represents Saturn in the Saturn-Venus dasha. There is some improvement in the dashamsha where Saturn is the lagna lord located in the eleventh house, and Venus is the yogakaraka occupying the tenth house. After Saturn-Venus was over, he sought re-election in November 2018 to a second Senate term and this time he was successful.

We have earlier discussed the chart (**chart 4**) of Mrs Indira Gandhi. She had imposed national emergency in India for almost twenty-one months (from June 25, 1975 to March 21, 1977) which had earned her the reputation of a dictator. The process started in Saturn-Mercury (November 17, 1973 to July 27, 1976). Satrun in exchange with the lagna lord is a mixed blessing. It gives rise to a rajayoga and is a potent malefic and maraka. Mercury is an adverse house lord associated with the Sun, aspected by another natural

Lagna	Ketu	Moon	
Sun Mercury	**Chart 22** February 26, 1958		
Venus			
Mars Saturn		Jup (R) Rahu	

Ketu
Sun
Mercury
2
10
1
11
Moon
Lagna
Venus
12
Mars
Saturn
3
9
6
4
8
5
7
Jup (R)
Rahu

Lagna	11°39'	Mars	23°06'	Venus	08°43'
Sun	14°11'	Mercury	09°44'	Saturn	01°18'
Moon	10°54'	Jupiter (R)	08°11'	Rahu	09°33'

Venus	Moon Saturn		Ketu
Sun	**Navamsha**		
Mercury Jup (R) Rahu		Lagna Mars	

9
Mer
Jup (R)
Rahu
8
Lagna
Mars
6
5
7
10
4
1
11
3
Sun
Moon
Saturn
Ketu
12
2
Venus

	Moon	Mercury	Sun
Lagna	**Dashamsha**		Mars Ketu
Rahu			
Jup (R) Saturn	Venus		

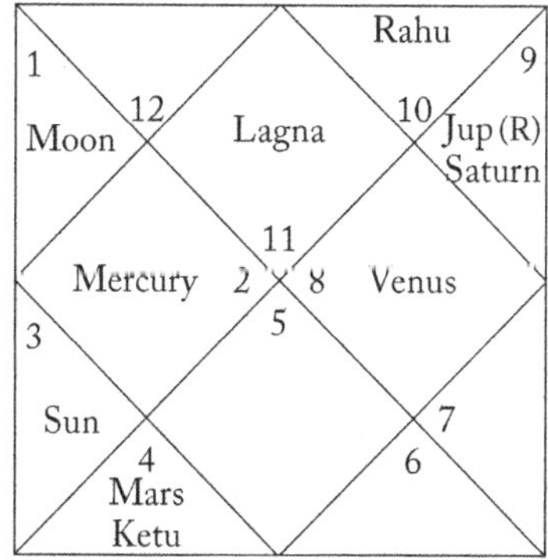

malefic Mars, as also by a retrograde sixth lord Jupiter, and occupying the fifth house of authority. In the general elections which were held after the lifting of emergency in March 1977, she lost miserably and a new government took over in India. This was in her Saturn-Ketu (July 27, 1976 to September 5, 1977) period. In September 1977, her dasha of Saturn-Venus (September 5, 1977 to November 4, 1980) started and things started improving for her. She manipulated the fall of the incumbent government and got it replaced by a government which her party supported from outside. Soon, the fall of the new government was also engineered and general elections were held in January 1980 when she came back to power with a vengeance. In between, there were several ups and downs but the final result was that she was back in the seat of power. Saturn as a kendra lord in exchange with the lagna lord has the potential to deliver raja-yoga results. Venus, the antardasha lord, does it eminently for Saturn, including the manipulations one expects from the eighth house lordship of Saturn. It may be noted that Venus is involved in an exchange between the sixth and eleventh lords. She connived with her erstwhile enemies (sixth house) to derive political advantage (eleventh house) against her current opponents. Saturn is quite strong in the navamsha and dashamsha charts and Venus has to deliver the results of Saturn during the Saturn-Venus dasha.

We have seen several charts with Saturn-Venus dasha operating at critical junctures. Let us now see the results of Venus-Saturn dasha also. **Chart 23** (male native, born on December 8, 1948, at 17:30 hours IST in Delhi, India) belongs to an Indian politician. He has been an important face in Delhi of a prominent political party of India. The native was running Venus-Saturn dasha (January 1, 2018 to March 3, 2021) when the elections to the Delhi Assembly

	Rahu	Lagna	
Moon	**Chart 23 (M)** December 8, 1948		
			Saturn
Mars Jupiter	Sun Mercury	Venus Ketu	

Rahu
3 4 Lagna 1 12
2
Saturn 5 11 Moon
8
6 Sun Mercury 10
7 Venus Ketu
9 Mars Jupiter

Lagna	25°36'	Mars	15°41'	Venus	22°12'
Sun	23°11'	Mercury	20°47'	Saturn	12°59'
Moon	22°18'	Jupiter	11°50'	Rahu	10°53'

	Moon Venus		
	Navamsha		Jup Sat Rahu
Sun Mercury Ketu			Lagna Mars

Jup Sat Rahu
6 7 Lagna Mars 4 3
5
8 2
11
1
9 Moon Venus
10 12
Sun Mer Ketu

Jupiter		Mars Venus	
Sun	**Dashamsha**		Rahu
Mercury Ketu			
Saturn			Lagna Moon

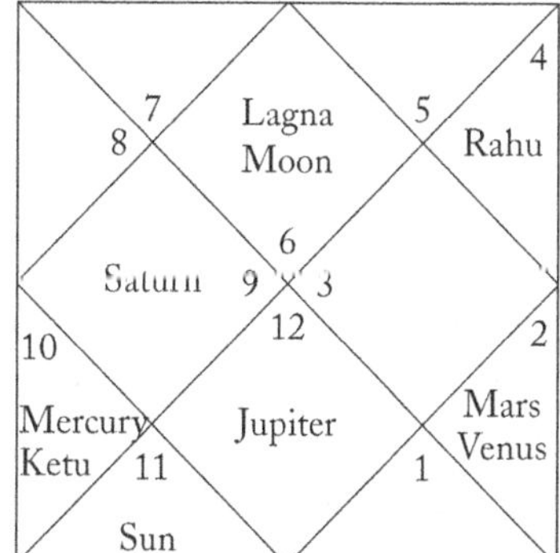

were held on February 8, 2019. The AD lord Saturn is supposed to give the results indicated by Venus. In this chart, Venus, the adverse sixth lord, occupies the sixth house along with another malefic, Ketu. The period was obviously not favourable and he lost badly in the elections. Venus is a functional malefic in the navamsha where it additionally receives the aspect of a highly malefic Saturn from the twelfth house. In the dashamsha chart, Venus, while in a favourable house, associates with the highly malefic third and eighth lord Mars.

Bahvartha Ratnakar on mutual Venus-Saturn dashas

The classic *Bhavartha Ratnakara* has this to say about the mutual MD/AD of Venus and Saturn:

शुक्रान्तरे शनेर्दाये शुक्रदाये तथा शने।
अन्तर्दशायां संप्राप्ते योगहीनो भवेन्नरः॥

शनिर्दाये तु शुक्रस्तु शुक्रदाये शनिस्तथा।
मीने धनुषि जातस्य योगदो भवति ध्रुवम्॥

That is: "The person becomes unfortunate during Saturn's mahadasha and Venus' antardasha, or Venus' mahadasha and Saturn's antardasha.

"For persons born in Dhanu and Meena lagnas, Venus and Saturn give rise to yoga (benefic results) in the dashas of Saturn and Venus respectively."

Thus, according to the *Bhavartha Ratnakara*, the lagnas of Jupiter are exempt from the general rule laid down by the *Laghu Parashari*. The facts may not be as simple as this. We have seen above that, in **chart 22**, the lagna is Meena but the Saturn-Venus dasha did not give any great results. Perhaps we need to consider the attending qualifications of the grahas as we have done all along during our analysis of the charts.

Uttara Kalamrita on mutual Venus-Saturn dashas

The *Uttara Kalamrita* of Kalidasa has something special to say about mutual dasha-antardashas of Venus and Saturn. Here are the two relevant shlokas:

भृग्वार्कौ यदि तुङ्गभे स्वभवने वर्गोत्तमादौ स्थितौ ।
तुल्यौ योगकरौ तथैव बलिनौ तौ चेन्मिथौ पाकगौ ॥

भूपालो धनदोपमोऽपि सततं भिक्षाशनो निष्फलः ।
तत्रैकस्तु बली परस्तु विबलश्चेद्वीर्यवान्योगदः ॥

तौ द्वावप्यबलौ व्ययाष्टरिपुगौ तद्भावपौ वाऽपि तत् ।
तद्भावेशयुतौ तदा शुभकरौ सौख्यप्रदौ भोगदौ ॥

एकः सद्भवनाधिपस्तदपरश्चेद्दुष्टभावेश्वर-
स्तावप्यत्र सुयोगदावतिखलौ तौ चेन्महासौख्यदौ ॥

That is: "If Venus and Saturn are in exaltation, in their own house or vargottama, and strong, and equally qualified to give rise to yoga, then in their mutual dasha-antardasha, they can render even a king of Kubera's stature a beggar and a failure. If one of them is weak and the other strong, the latter is capable of producing yoga.

"If both Venus and Saturn are weak, located in houses 6, 8 or 12, or owning these houses, or associated with these house lords, then they give benefic results, providing happiness and enjoyments. If one (of them) owns a benefic house and the other a malefic house, then too they give benefic results. If both are malefic, then too they give highly beneficial results."

The rules of Kalidasa about the mutual MD/AD of Saturn and Venus appear a little strange but do need some exploration. When both Venus and Saturn are equally strong, their mutual dashas tend to be problematic. We have discussed above the chart of Paul Ryan (chart 21) who has Saturn debilitated and his Saturn-Venus did prove to be auspicious.

लग्नकर्माधिनेतारावन्योन्याश्रयसंस्थितौ ।
राजयोगाविति प्रोक्तं विख्यातो विजयी भवेत् ॥ 41 ॥

धर्मकर्माधिनेतारावन्योन्याश्रयसंस्थितौ ।
राजयोगाविति प्रोक्तं विख्यातो विजयी भवेत् ॥ 42 ॥

41. When the lagna lord and the tenth lord occupy one or the other of these houses, the resulting (two) yogas ensure wide renown and success for the native.

42. When the ninth lord and the tenth lord occupy one or the other of these houses, the resulting (two) yogas ensure wide renown and success for the native.

Comments: Four different yogas are mentioned here. They all ensure success and fame for the native. They are:

1. Lagna lord and tenth lord in the lagna;
2. Lagna lord and tenth lord in the tenth house;
3. Ninth lord and tenth lord in the ninth house;
4. Ninth lord and tenth lord in the tenth house.

We have known pretty well by now that the combination of a trikona lord with a kendra lord produces a great rajayoga. In these two verses, the yogas mentioned are quite understandable. Any link between the lagna lord and the tenth lord produces a rajayoga. The tenth house is the strongest kendra and the lagna is the most auspicious house by virtue of its being both a kendra and a trikona.

The lagna lord has the capacity to neutralise the adverse effects of even the eighth house lordship. The placement of the two lords in any of these auspicious houses adds to their beneficence. Similarly any link between the lord of the strongest trikona, the ninth house, with the strongest kendra lord again produces a highly auspicious yoga that promises all renown and success. The placement of these two house lords in these very auspicious houses adds to their beneficence. We would like to believe that these yogas would give results when the lords of the houses mentioned are themselves untainted by adverse house lordship or the aspects of adverse house lords. We have earlier seen in **chart 7** a conjunction of the ninth lord Jupiter and the tenth lord Mars in the ninth house, further fortified by the association of the lagna lord Moon. However, this great yoga is tainted to some extent by the simultaneous lordship of the sixth house by Jupiter and the aspect on this combination of the eighth lord Saturn from the twelfth house.

Chart 24 (male native, born on May 30, 1952, at 13:00 hours IST, in Delhi, India) belongs to a reputed physician in India. The lagna lord Sun and the tenth lord Venus occupy the tenth house forming a great rajayoga. The association

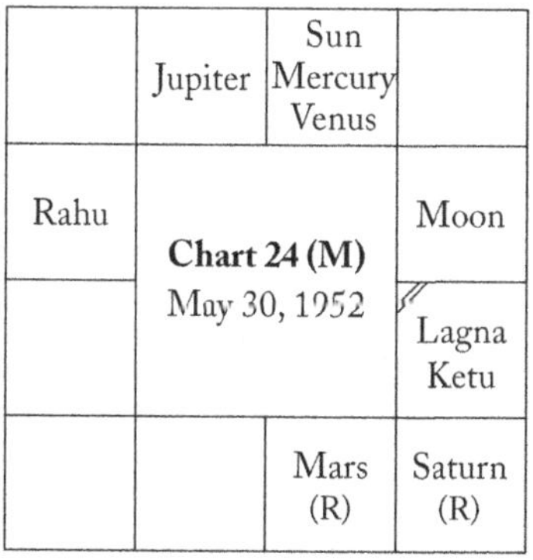

	Jupiter	Sun Mercury Venus	
Rahu	**Chart 24 (M)** May 30, 1952		Moon
			Lagna Ketu
		Mars (R)	Saturn (R)

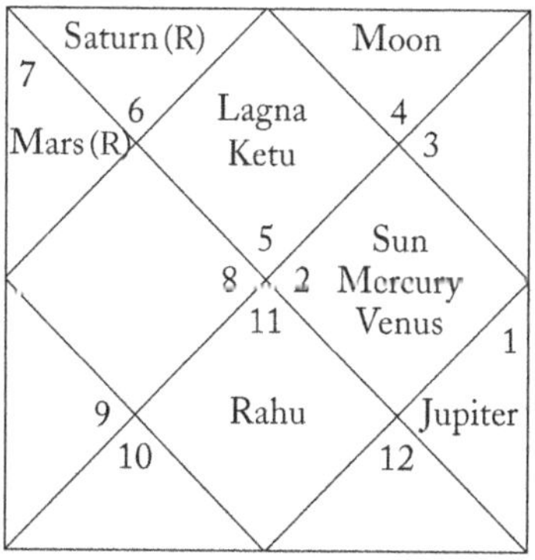

Saturn (R)
Moon
7
6
Lagna Ketu
4
3
Mars (R)
5
Sun Mercury Venus
8
2
11
1
9
Rahu
Jupiter
10
12

Lagna	25°46'	Mars (R)	08°45'	Venus	08°39'
Sun	15°37'	Mercury	04°05'	Saturn (R)	15°06'
Moon	28°12'	Jupiter	14°06'	Rahu	01°21'

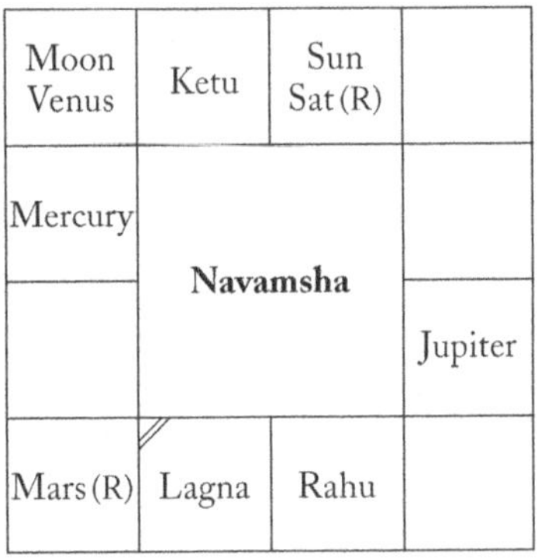

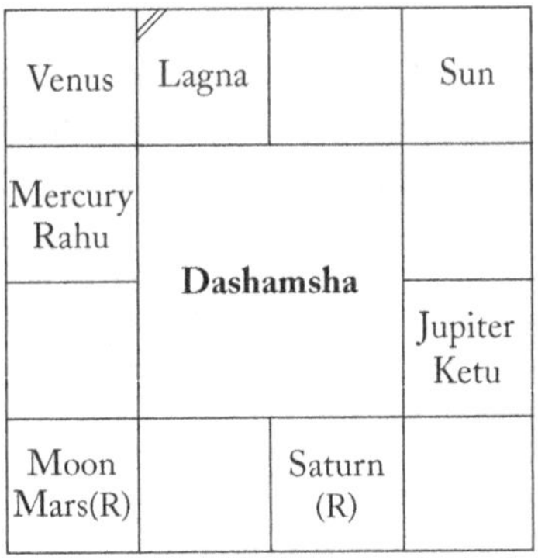

Moon Venus	Ketu	Sun Sat (R)	
Mercury	**Navamsha**		
			Jupiter
Mars (R)	Lagna	Rahu	

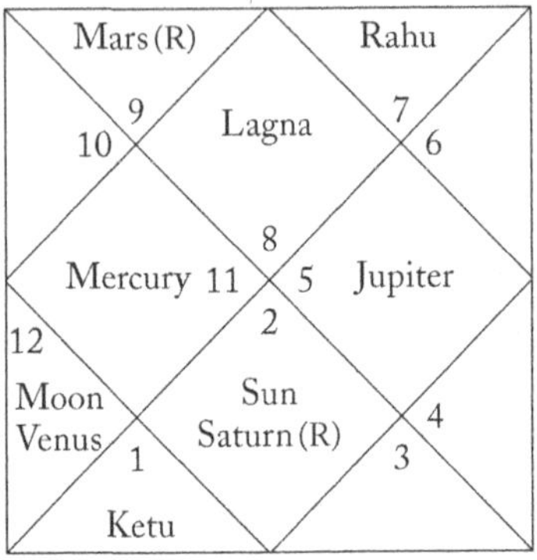

Mars (R) Rahu
9 Lagna 7
10 6
8
Mercury 11 5 Jupiter
2
12
Moon Sun
Venus Saturn (R) 4
1 3
Ketu

Venus	Lagna		Sun
Mercury Rahu	**Dashamsha**		
			Jupiter Ketu
Moon Mars(R)		Saturn (R)	

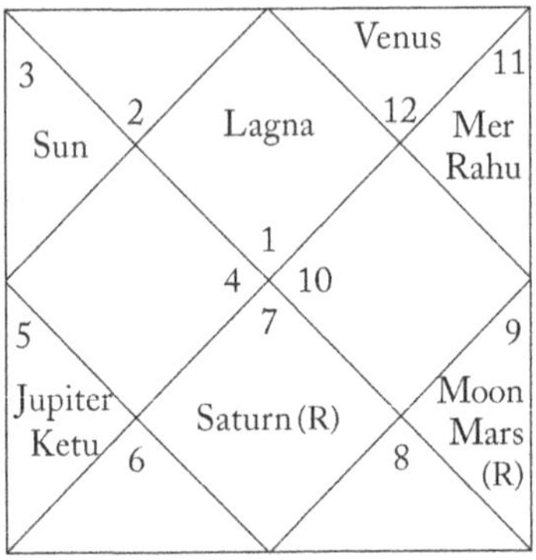

Venus
11
3
2 Lagna 12 Mer
Sun Rahu
1
4 10
7
5 9
Jupiter Saturn (R) Moon
Ketu 6 8 Mars
(R)

of Mercury, the second and the eleventh lord, modifies it into a significant dhana-yoga (yoga for money). However, the rajayoga is itself tainted by the third house lordship of Venus, and further by the eleventh house lordship of Mercury. Mars, the yogakaraka, also aspects this yoga. There are other positive aspects to this chart in that the lagna, with Ketu in it, receives the aspect of Jupiter from the ninth house, and the mutual disposition of the Moon and Jupiter gives rise to a Gaja-Kesari yoga. The sum total of all this is good name and a good amount of money earned through legitimate means. There is a lot of 'Sun' influence on the tenth house. The lagna lord Sun in the tenth house associates with Mercury and Venus, both in the nakshatra of the Sun, that too Krittika, all indicating a profession concerned with healing.

We have seen above the combination of the lagna lord with the tenth lord in the tenth house, with some modifications. We shall now see the role of the tenth lord and the ninth lord together in the ninth or the tenth house. In **chart 25** (male native, born on September 14, 1955 at 16:05 hours IST, in Saharanpur, UP, India), the lagna is Makara with the lagna lord forming a potent Shasha yoga by its exaltation in the tenth house. An exalted Jupiter in the seventh house forms the Hamsa yoga and further strengthens the lagna by its aspect. The ninth house is occupied by the ninth lord Mercury and the tenth lord Venus. The native is a renowned academician and a reputed orthopaedic surgeon. The fifth (education) and the tenth (profession) lord, Venus, here too resides in the nakshatra of the Sun. The restrictions posed on this yoga include a Paapa-Kartari yoga around the ninth house where this great combination of Venus and Mercury exists, and the simultaneous lordship of the sixth house by Mercury. The affliction of the seventh house (by Saturn's aspect), and of the seventh lord in the eighth house, leads to chronic ill health for his wife.

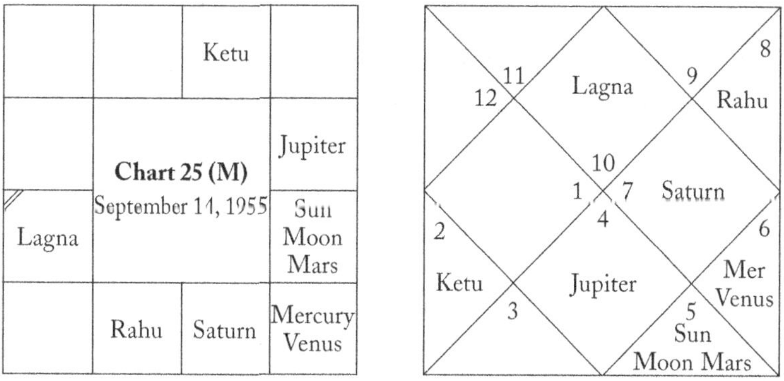

		Ketu	
	Chart 25 (M)		Jupiter
Lagna	September 14, 1955		Sun Moon Mars
	Rahu	Saturn	Mercury Venus

12 11 Lagna 9 8 Rahu
10
1 7 Saturn
4
2 6
Ketu Jupiter Mer Venus
3 5
Sun Moon Mars

Lagna	11°53'	Mars	18°13'	Venus	01°09'
Sun	27°35'	Mercury	23°42'	Saturn	23°46'
Moon	04°28'	Jupiter	26°40'	Rahu	28°56'

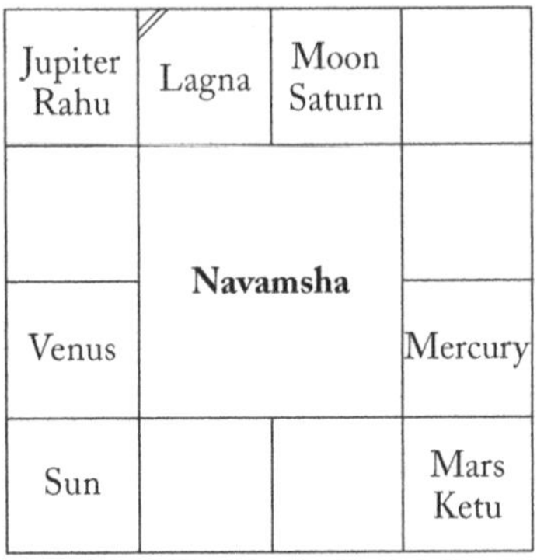

Jupiter Rahu	Lagna	Moon Saturn	
	Navamsha		
Venus			Mercury
Sun			Mars Ketu

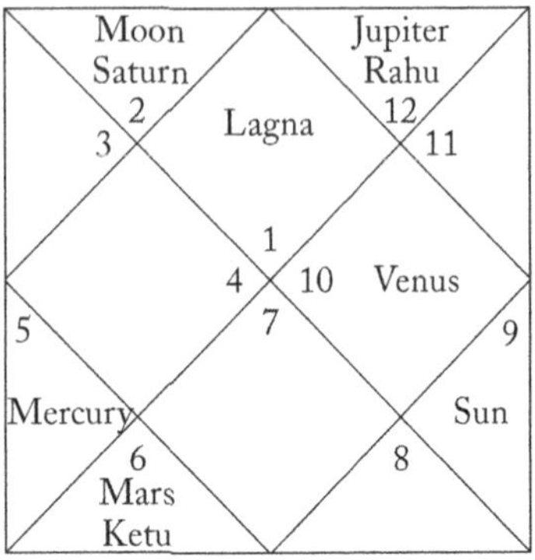

Moon Saturn 2 3
Lagna
Jupiter Rahu 12 11
1
4 10 Venus
7
5 9
Mercury
Sun
6 Mars Ketu
8

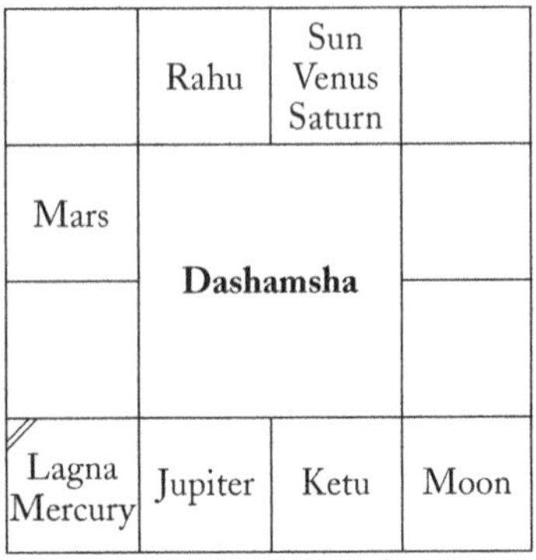

	Rahu	Sun Venus Saturn	
Mars	**Dashamsha**		
Lagna Mercury	Jupiter	Ketu	Moon

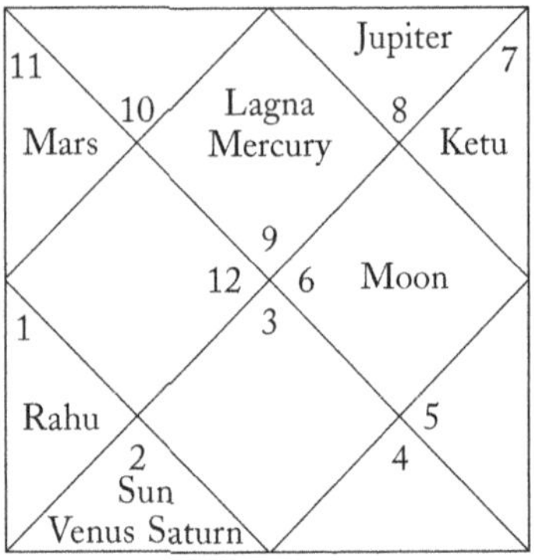

11
Mars 10
Lagna Mercury
Jupiter 8 7
Ketu
9
12 6 Moon
3
1
Rahu
5
2 Sun Venus Saturn
4

Another much stronger combination of the ninth and tenth lords, this time in the tenth house, exists in **chart 26** (male native, born on July 27, 1947, at 10:06 hours IST, Delhi, India) with Kanya lagna. The combination here too consists of Venus and Mercury. Neither Venus nor Mercury owns any adverse house. Mercury actually happens to be the lagna lord hence providing further strength to this yoga. The combination in the tenth house also receives the aspect of Jupiter which too does not own any of the adverse houses. This is a highly clean, unadulterated benefic yoga in the tenth house. Our classic grants to such a native great renown and success over his opponents. Mercury and Venus remain significant in the navamsha and dashamsha charts also, particularly Venus which gets exalted in the dashamsha.

		Mars Rahu	Mercury Venus
	Chart 26 (M) July 27, 1947		Sun Saturn
	Moon Ketu	Jupiter	Lagna

Jupiter
8
7
Moon
Ketu
Lagna
5
4
Sun
Saturn
6
9
3
12
Mercury
Venus
2
10
11
Mars
Rahu
1

Lagna	07°05'	Mars	25°00'	Venus	29°41'
Sun	10°11'	Mercury	24°02'	Saturn	18°05'
Moon	05°50'	Jupiter	24°45'	Rahu	07°32'

Lagna Rahu		Mercury Jupiter	Venus
	Navamsha		
			Moon Mars
Saturn		Sun	Ketu

2
Mer
Jupiter
1
Lagna
Rahu
11
10
12
Venus
3
9
Saturn
6
4
Ketu
8
5
Moon
Mars
7
Sun

Venus Rahu			Sun Jupiter
Mercury	**Dashamsha**		Lagna
			Moon
			Mars Saturn Ketu

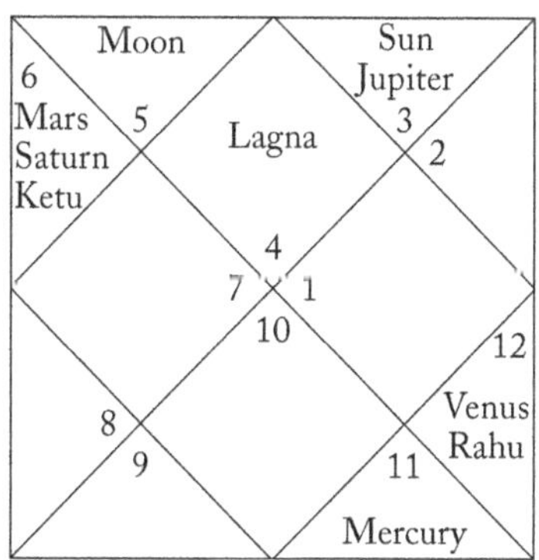

One might spot the blemish of a Paapa-Kartari yoga around the tenth house, thus restricting the expression of the yoga only to some extent. The native is a qualified mechanical engineer from India who further qualified in industrial engineering in the USA and entered the world of business. He has earned millions through sheer hard work and has taken up charity and philanthropy on a large scale. He has made generous donations toward the cause of health. His business acumen and passion for excellence has made him a leading businessman in the USA. The benevolent yoga obtaining in the tenth house, the house of Karma, aspected by a benevolent Jupiter, only ensures good intentions and great achievements.

While we have been discussing the conjunctions, it is understandable that even an exchange between the lagna lord and the tenth lord, and an exchange between the ninth lord and the tenth lord, would also produce some powerful rajayogas. In fact some other authors have taken the two above shlokas under consideration to respectively mean: "*When the tenth lord occupies the lagna and the lagna lord occupies the tenth house, it leads to a rajayoga ensuring renown and success.*" And "*When the ninth lord occupies the tenth house and the tenth lord occupies the ninth house, it leads to a rajayoga ensuring renown and success.*" However, the constitution of the shlokas indicates the meanings that we have provided, and that each shloka indicates the occurrence of two yogas, not just the one indicating an exchange.

Still others opine the above shlokas to respectively mean as follows: "*When the lagna lord and the tenth lord either exchange houses or are together in one of these two houses, the resulting (two) yogas ensure wide renown and success to the native.*" And "*When the ninth lord and the tenth lord either exchange houses or are together in one of these two houses, the resulting (two) yogas ensure wide renown and success to the native.*"

As has been our method of analysis all along, the corollary of the above would be the following additional rajayogas produced by the interaction of different house lords:

1. Lagna lord and fourth lord;
2. Lagna lord and fifth lord;
3. Lagna lord and seventh lord;
4. Lagna lord and ninth lord;
5. Ninth lord and fourth lord;
6. Ninth lord and seventh lord.

These yogas would be produced when the two house lords mentioned in any of the yogas above together occupy one of the two houses. Their exchanges too would be effective rajayogas. It must be stated that all these rajayogas would ensure name and fame for the native but would not be as strong as the four yogas explained earlier in the shlokas under consideration.

CHAPTER 7

The Realm of the Laghu Parashari

The *Laghu Parashari* is a condensed classic which conceals within its body several profound principles of Vedic astrology. There are forty-two shlokas or Sanskrit verses only, each shloka subsuming in its body profound meaning. The division into six chapters is rather arbitrary with some overlap of the subjects mentioned in each chapter. We have preserved the division into chapters though the English translation of the names of the chapters is not too exact. It is a marvellous work on the methods of analysis of one of the most wonderful nakshatra-based dashas in Vedic astrology, the Vimshottari dasha. The Vimshottari is a dasha with a duration of one hundred and twenty years. The author makes it absolutely clear in the very beginning that the principles mentioned here apply only to the Vimshottari dasha and to none other (shloka 3). He specifically mentions that these principles are not to be applied to the Ashtottari, another popular dasha of Parashara with a duration of one hundred and eight years.

Another point that the author clarifies is that the student must acquire the knowledge of the basics of astrology from the available standard texts (shloka 4). He does not want to waste his time on the fundamentals. Knowledge about the fundamentals is essential but the author has chosen to confine himself to very specific aspects of the subject here. It is thus essential that knowledge about the houses, rashis, grahas, nakshatras, vargas and even the calculation of the Vimshottari dasha be acquired from the available, popular, standard texts on Vedic astrology. We have clarified some of the basics of Vedic astrology in the early pages of this work for the convenience of the reader. An understanding of those basics is necessary to comprehend the principles enshrined in this classic. The discerning student may find it further useful to refer to more advanced works on the subject to be able to fully appreciate the worth and beauty of this outstanding, condensed presentation on Vedic astrology.

About the vargas

The vargas or divisional charts must always be studied along with the rashi chart. The navamsha must always be studied in any chart analysis. It is said that the promise inherent in the rashi chart must be confirmed in the navamsha chart before making any prediction. Authorities have gone so far as to say that if there is a conflict between the indications from the rashi chart and the navamsha chart, the latter takes precedence. Since this classic is primarily concerned with the rajayogas, we find it appropriate to study the dashamsha chart also, besides the rashi and the navamsha, in most of the examples. Some other charts, like the drekkana and the dwadashamsha, have been referred to in the chapter on the determination of longevity. These two charts must also be studied when dealing with rashi charts indicating health issues. The drekkana is especially relevant to matters of health. The twenty-second drekkana, which corresponds to the eighth house of the drekkana chart, is highly relevant to any serious illness. Even the sixth house of the drekkana chart and its lord are important in matters of health and disease.

Aspects

All grahas exert their influence on other grahas and houses through their associations or aspects. All grahas cast their full glance on their seventh house and the grahas located there. The outer planets, i.e., Mars, Jupiter and Saturn, have their special aspects. Mars fully aspects houses 4, 7 and 8; Jupiter fully aspects houses 5, 7 and 9; Saturn fully aspects houses 3, 7 and 10 (shloka 5). Our classic only recognises the full aspects. The partial aspects described by sage Parashara in the *Brihat Parashara Hora Shastra* (*BPHS*) have no role in the formation of yogas according to the *Laghu Parashari*.

Classification of grahas

This classic gives importance to the functional nature of grahas. Eventually, it is the functional nature of a graha which determines the nature of results it confers on the native. The functional nature of a graha is dependent on the house lordship of the graha, which in turn depends on the lagna. The following classes of grahas are mentioned here:

Trikona (houses 5 and 9) lords:	Ever benefic;
Kendra (houses 4, 7, 10) lords:	Neither benefic nor malefic;
Lords of tri-shad-aaya:	Ever malefic;
Lords of houses 2 and 12:	Impressionable neutrals;
Lord of the eighth house:	Highly malefic; and
The lagna lord:	Having a special benefic nature.

The kendras, the trikonas and the 3-6-11 houses are considered to be progressively stronger. This means that the ninth house is the strongest trikona, the tenth house the strongest kendra and the eleventh house the strongest in maleficence. The blemish of the eighth house lordship is not supposed to apply to the Sun and the Moon. It is possible that no blemish is attached to the Sun and the

Moon as eighth lords when they participate in the rajayogas, which is the main subject of this classic. However, in medical astrology at least, the eighth house lordship of the Sun and the Moon almost certainly proves to be adverse for the native's health.

The above classification is slightly at variance with the *BPHS*. The sage in the *BPHS* holds that the houses 2, 12 and 8 are neutral though he hastens to add that the eighth house has a special evil propensity because of its being the twelfth from the ninth! Also in the *BPHS*, the lagna is considered among both the kendras and trikonas. Since the kendras and the trikonas are progressively stronger, the lagna, according to the *BPHS*, is the weakest among the kendras and also weakest among the trikonas.

About the kendra lords

The kendra lords on their own are neither benefic nor malefic. Kendras have a neutralising influence over their lords. If the graha owning a kendra is a natural malefic, it loses its maleficence. If it happens to be a natural benefic, it sheds its beneficence. While natural benefics as lords of the kendras lose their beneficence, their placement in the kendras is always considered beneficial. In case of natural malefics as lords of kendras, there is loss of their maleficence but their placement in the kendras is not considered benefic. So a distinction has to be made between lordship and placement.

When a natural malefic owns a kendra, it merely sheds its maleficence. It needs to additionally own a benefic house, a trikona, to actually become a functional benefic (shloka 12). Mars and Saturn thus become functional benefics for Karka and Simha lagnas in the case of the former and for Vrisha and Tula lagnas in the case of the latter. In these situations, they are called yoga-karakas (shloka 17).

Kendraadhipatya dosha

This is the blemish that applies to the natural benefics when they happen to own the kendra houses (shlokas 10 and 11). The blemish is supposed to be most severe for Jupiter followed by Venus, Mercury and the Moon in that order. It may be noted that in case of the lagna belonging to Jupiter or Mercury, each graha would own two kendras. It is presumed that the blemish would be either less or non-existent if the graha owns the lagna as one of the kendras. If any of these grahas happens to occupy its kendra house, it gives rise to a potent Pancha-Mahapurusha yoga and the blemish must diminish substantially.

The adverse houses

Tri-shad-aaya or houses 3, 6 and 11 are considered to be ever malefic (shloka 6). We have seen in the examples discussed above that the lordship of these houses destroys, spoils or adulterates the rajayogas formed by their lords when they simultaneously own a benefic house. For a good yoga to deliver unflinching benevolent results, its constituent grahas should not own any of the houses 3, 6 and 11, and even house 8 (chart 2). The *BPHS* also mentions Trika houses. The Trika houses are houses 6, 8 and 12. They are considered to be adverse houses and their lords to be adverse grahas. The *Laghu Parashari* stays away from using the term Trika and continues to consider house 12 as neutral as far as the formation of rajayogas is concerned.

We would like to elaborate on these houses a little bit more. The third is the house of physical fitness and courage. The sixth is the house of competition and resistance against enemies and disease. The eleventh is the house of monetary gains, achievements and recovery from illness. All these three houses and their lords are supposed to be important in the present day context. We have a world where there is stiff competition in life and a fight for survival. We need strength to resist disease and enemies. And we need money and recognition in life to live respectably in the modern world. All these aspects of life may have been an impediment to the spiritual progress of an individual but they are important for those who live in this material world. The times of Parashara were spiritual times. Materialism was not much appreciated in that era. The eleventh house, though considered the most malefic of the houses, is particularly important in the formation of dhana yogas (combinations for wealth and prosperity). When rajayogas involve the eleventh house lord, the rise in status is also associated with monetary gains, whether fair or foul (charts 4, 6, 11, 14, 24). Even rajayogas forming in the eleventh house raise the income and financial status of the individual (charts 18, 20).

We may also add a comment about the eighth house here. The maleficence of the eighth house is due to its falling in the twelfth from the ninth (shloka 9). Being the house of longevity, it, by implication, is the house of death as well. In daily life, the eighth is the house of scandals. However, it is also the house for inheritance, enigmatic earnings and underground wealth. Deep research also comes under the realm of the eighth house. The student of astrology is advised to seriously consider these positive aspects of some of the malefic houses while interpreting the yogas.

The formation of yogas

Different grades of rajayogas form by the mutual interaction or interconnectedness of the kendra and trikona lords. When the kendra and trikona lords conjoin, without them having any adverse qualifications, special benefic and auspicious yogas result, producing an individual who is famous, dignified and benevolent (shloka 14). Even those strong kendra and trikona lords which are even somewhat blemished produce rajayogas by their mere interconnectedness (shloka 15). Smt Indira Gandhi (chart 4) continued to enjoy rajayogas during the mahadashas of Jupiter (involving an exchange between the fourth/eleventh lord Venus and the sixth/ninth lord Jupiter) and Saturn (involving exchange between the lagna lord Moon and the seventh/eighth lord Saturn). The blemishes of the yoga-producing grahas are the simultaneous lordship of the tri-shad-aaya houses. The interconnectedness is of any of the four types already discussed under the comments to shloka 14. Any association or relationship between the ninth and tenth lords also produces rajayogas (shloka 16). This relationship may be by association, by exchange of houses or even when *either house lord is located in the other's house*. This latter condition emphasises the link of a graha with a house. The ninth is the strongest trikona and the tenth the strongest kendra. The location of the ninth lord in the tenth house, according to this definition, produces a rajayoga as does the placement of the tenth lord in the ninth house. The principle can be suitably extended to the other kendras and trikonas.

Shloka 17 states that a rajayoga would result if a strong kendra lord establishes any relationship with a trikona lord or a strong trikona lord establishes relationship with a kendra lord. The strength to be considered here is not the strength based on the house owned by the graha but on its actual strength in terms of exaltation, own house placement, moolatrikona placement and strength in the navamsha (vargottama, exaltation, etc.). In chart 6, we have a conjunction of Mars and Venus in the ninth house for Karka lagna. Mars is the lord of a trikona (fifth house) along with that of the strongest kendra, the tenth house. Venus is a kendra (fourth house) lord exalted in the ninth house.

An exception in the formation of rajayogas by mutual interrelationship of the ninth and tenth lords is mentioned in shloka 22. It says that the rajayoga fails to fructify if these two house lords also own the eighth house or the eleventh house. Consistently in this text, the eighth house lord has been held as the most malefic. The eleventh house lord is the most malefic of the tri-shad-aaya group. This situation can happen with either Mesha lagna or Mithuna lagna where Saturn and Jupiter fail to produce yoga because Saturn owns the eleventh house in one case and the eighth in the other. As usual, extending this principle to other kendras, trikonas and the tri-shad-aaya group, yogas would fail to fructify if kendra and trikona lords simultaneously happen to either own the eighth house or one of the 3, 6 and 11 houses. The examples we have discussed show abundantly that the results get modified when additional qualifications attend upon the yoga-producing grahas.

It may also be noted that grahas which own two houses, one a trikona and the other either the second or the twelfth house, the latter being considered neutral houses, do not earn any blemish of owning either a maraka house or a Trika house according to this classic. Thus Mars for Dhanu lagna, Venus for Mithuna lagna, Mercury for Tula lagna and Jupiter for Mesha lagna remain benefic because of owning a trikona and a neutral house in each case.

Yoga-karaka graha

A graha that owns both a kendra and a trikona is called a yogakaraka. A yogakaraka has special benevolence attached to it. The benevolence of the yogakaraka gets enhanced many times if it additionally establishes any relationship with another trikona lord (shloka 20). As we have already clarified, Mars is the yogakaraka for Karka and Simha lagnas, Venus for Makara and Kumbha lagnas, and Saturn for Vrisha and Tula lagnas. Charts 5, 7 and 25 are good examples of a yogakaraka associating with another trikona lord and giving good results. In chart 8 (Marilyn Monroe) too, there is a conjunction of a yogakaraka with another trikona lord, forming a potent rajayoga, but it is blemished by its location in the eighth house, and the native, as a consequence, remained mired in intrigues and scandals involving highly placed individuals.

Yoga-karaka dashas

Shlokas 18 and 19 point to some very subtle and sensitive principles of dasha interpretation. These shlokas seem to be generally misunderstood and misinterpreted. We have already explained these shlokas with appropriate examples. However, we feel that these shlokas, because of their peculiar significance in understanding the subtleties involved, need further elucidation even at the risk of some repetition.

According to shloka 18, the yogakaraka (maha-)dashas often give desirable results. But the mahadasha has to deliver its results during the antardashas that operate within it. The principles mentioned in these two shlokas, concerning the antardashas operating within a yogakaraka mahadasha, are:

- Between two yogakaraka antardashas, the intervening antardashas of benefics *unrelated with* the mahadasha lord also yield good results; and
- Between two yogakaraka antardashas, the intervening antardashas of malefics *related with* the mahadasha lord also yield good results.

Thus, in both situations, good results will be experienced. However, in the case of an intervening benefic antardasha, the AD lord does not have to be related to the MD lord whereas in the case of an intervening malefic antardasha, the AD lord needs to be related to the MD lord. The reason is explained in a subsequent shloka (shloka 30). There it is mentioned that the MD lord gives its results during the AD of those grahas which are either related to it or are if its own inherent nature. During the mahadasha of a yogakaraka, a benefic antardasha lord does not need to be related to the MD lord to produce good results because it is of the nature of the MD lord, a benefic. If a benefic AD lord were related to a yogakaraka MD, it would certainly produce good results. In the case of a malefic AD lord, the maleficence can be neutralised only if the AD lord gets related to the benefic MD lord and thus sheds its maleficence through benefic influence. There is also another principle here. Between two yogakaraka antardashas, an adverse antardasha behaves like a malefic graha in a Shubha-Kartari yoga. We have seen earlier, in chart 5, that during the mahadasha of an exalted lagna lord Saturn, two good antardashas of Mercury and Venus came into operation at a crucial juncture in the career of the native. The intervening adverse Saturn-Ketu dasha too continued the good effects and acted like a good bridge between two good antardashas.

In chart 6 also, the same principle is illuminated. After joining politics, the native won three elections to the Lok Sabha, the lower house of the Indian Parliament, between 1984 and 1991. The dashas operating during that period were Jupiter-Saturn, Jupiter-Mercury, Jupiter-Ketu and Jupiter-Venus. Jupiter-Saturn does not need much explanation as it is the MD of a trikona lord and the AD of a kendra lord. Jupiter-Mercury is the AD of a malefic house lord in a highly malefic house. Jupiter-Ketu is the AD of a functionally benefic shadowy graha as it is located in a kendra and its dispositor is forming a great rajayoga in the ninth house. Additionally, it is under the aspect of the MD lord. Jupiter-Venus is the dasha of a trikona lord and a kendra lord, hence benefic. It is the intervening Jupiter-Mercury which could have created problems. However, Jupiter-Mercury falls between two favourable dashas and

Mercury is also related to the MD lord. This Mercury did not behave well during the Saturn-Mercury dasha when the presidency of the native concluded and he did not get an extension for another term. Saturn behaved as a malefic eighth lord and Mercury as an adverse house lord in the eighth house, exchanging houses with the eighth lord. Even as a yogakaraka mahadasha delivers its benefic effects during the antardashas of unrelated benefics or related malefics, so also a malefic mahadasha, like that of Saturn in this case, delivers its malefic effects during the antardashas of functional malefics, whether related to it, like Mercury related to Saturn by exchange in this case, or unrelated to it.

About longevity

This classic allots six shlokas to the subject of longevity. We have already provided sufficient explanations about those verses in the concerned chapter. Some additional comments are needed in the case of shloka 28 to lay stress on the importance of Saturn as a killer. This is not to frighten the reader. It needs to be emphasised, even at the risk of repetition, that the marakas or the 'killer' grahas do not kill unless the longevity is over. As long as the longevity is not over, their dashas (MD, AD, PD) can only disturb health.

The shloka under consideration states that a malefic Saturn, by its relationship with marakas, most certainly supersedes all other marakas and malefics as a killer. A malefic Saturn is a Saturn which owns adverse houses (houses 3, 6, 11 and 8). It tends to become a potent killer if it gets connected with other marakas or even malefics. In chart 19 (JFK), with Kanya lagna, Jupiter is a maraka. Saturn is not a maraka but the lord of an adverse house, the sixth. It is under a severe malefic influence of the eighth lord Mars. The native died in Jupiter-Saturn dasha.

Even a yogakaraka Saturn when under severe malefic influence can cause death during its dasha. In chart 17

(Benito Mussolini), the yogakaraka Saturn associates with a maraka Mars in a highly malefic house, the eighth, along with the tenth lord Moon. It was in the Saturn-Rahu period that the native was deposed and assassinated. Saturn, which is the karaka for longevity and considered good when located in the eighth house, of longevity, does not seem to protect longevity when it is afflicted in the eighth house. Also, dashas of grahas related to the lagna and the eighth house tend to cause the end of life when the longevity is over. Additionally, we have seen that the combined influence of Saturn and Mars on the eighth house, whether by association or aspect, tends to cause a violent or unexpected or painful death (charts 11, 17, 19) unless there is sufficient protection from natural benefics like Jupiter.

Rahu and Ketu – the shadowy grahas

Rahu and Ketu have been treated in this classic in three shlokas: 13, 21 and 36. They have their importance in the creation of important yogas and their dashas play important roles in the lives of the individuals.

In shloka 13, it is stated that Rahu and Ketu behave according to the house of their occupation and according to the graha they associate with. The matter is further clarified in shloka 21 and the example we have discussed in the comments. That they behave as the lord of the house they occupy is the reason why they produce rajayogas by associating with the kendra lords when they occupy the trikonas, and by associating with the trikona lords when they occupy the kendras. And they produce great results when they associate with key yoga-karaka grahas. We have seen this in chart 9 belonging to Princess Diana. Rahu in her tenth house associates with the lagna lord and qualifies for a yoga-karaka. Similarly, Ketu in the fourth house associates with the ninth lord Moon and qualifies as a yoga-karaka. She met Prince Charles first in Rahu-Moon dasha and got married to him in Rahu-Mars dasha. Rahu and Ketu thus assured her association with, and inclusion in, the royal family.

There is further clarification about the role of Rahu and Ketu in shloka 36. It is mentioned there that Rahu and Ketu in auspicious houses, which means the kendras and the trikonas, render yogakaraka results during the appropriate antardashas, provided these two grahas are not connected, and thus influenced, by other house lords. This fact is quite obvious in chart 18 belonging to Bill Clinton. Rahu in Vrisha in the ninth house is unassociated and unaspected, hence unaffected by any other graha. It is thus capable of giving yogakaraka results during the various antardashas that operate in its mahadasha. Rahu gave excellent results starting from the Rahu-Mercury dasha; Mercury is the lagna lord as well as the tenth lord.

The benevolence of Rahu in a kendra, uninfluenced by any other graha is further exemplified by chart 19 belonging to JFK. His Rahu is located in the fourth house in Dhanu, unassociated with any other graha and also unaspected by any. Rahu dasha proved to be a yogakaraka dasha for him. Before the Rahu mahadasha ended, he had become the President of the USA.

An important point that emerges here is worth consideration. All along in this classic, we have been stressing the importance of connectedness of the antardasha lord with the mahadasha lord. During the mahadasha of a yogakaraka, even a malefic antardasha lord gives good results when it happens to associate with the mahadasha lord. Not so with Rahu and Ketu. The author says that Rahu and Ketu give yogakaraka results when located in good houses provided they are not connected with any other graha. Only when they are not connected with another graha are they able to give good results unhindered. This appears to be an exception to the general rule.

We need to add here some information about Rahu and Ketu that sage Parashara provides in his *BPHS*. That information is as follows:

- Rahu gets exalted in Vrisha;
- Ketu gets exalted in Vrishchika;
- Moolatrikona rashi of Rahu is Mithuna;
- Moolatrikona rashi of Ketu is Dhanu;
- Rahu's own rashi is Kumbha;
- Ketu's own rashi is Vrishchika;
- Alternate view: Rahu owns Kanya, Ketu Meena.

Sage Parashara does not attribute any aspects to Rahu and Ketu. As a consequence, we have considered here only association with either Rahu or Ketu, or the involvement of a graha or a house in the Rahu-Ketu axis (RKA).

Results of dashas

As is well understood, grahas give their results when their dashas are in operation. A mahadasha lord is the main deciding factor about what all may happen during its period extending over several years. However, it does not give its expected results during its own antardasha (shloka 29). The good or bad results of a mahadasha lord are experienced during the dashas of those grahas which are either related with the mahadasha lord or are of its own 'Dharma' or inherent nature (shloka 30). A yogakaraka mahadasha lord will thus give its yogakaraka results during the dashas of those benefics which are either related or unrelated with it; it will give similar results during the antardashas of malefics if they happen to be related with it; and it will give similar results during the antardashas of those grahas which are of its own nature even if unrelated. The same will be true about the mahadashas of malefics. In case of antardasha lords which are not related to the mahadasha lord and which are likely to give results contrary to the mahadasha lord, the wise astrologer must use all his wisdom and knowledge and understanding of the subject to deduce the correct outcome (shloka 31). In general, good results are to be expected during the mahadasha of a kendra lord in the antardasha of a trikona lord, or during the mahadasha of a trikona lord in the antardasha of a kendra lord, provided the two are connected with each other; not so if they are not mutually connected (shloka 32). We have already explained some of these principles above.

An important principle of dasha interpretation is mentioned in shloka 33. It says that a rajayoga that begins during the antardasha of a maraka gets further support during subsequent malefic antardashas provided those antardasha lords are connected with the mahadasha lord. The principle is well exemplified in the case of chart 18 (Bill Clinton). The native became the Governor of Arkansas during the later part of Rahu-Venus dasha, Rahu in the ninth house and Venus the ninth lord. He had earlier lost during the same dasha but the Neecha-Bhanga of Venus came to his rescue and ensured his success eventually. Venus is a maraka, being the lord of the second house. This yoga that fructified during the antardasha of a malefic continued during the subsequent antardashas and he remained the Governor of Arkansas for four successive terms, well into the Jupiter mahadasha. Jupiter is a maraka too and the rajayoga continued during its own antardasha and during subsequent antardashas as well.

About shloka 35: The text says that during the mahadasha of a benefic, the antardasha of a related yogakaraka occasionally gives rajayoga. This does not seem to be unusual. However, the alternate version, which says that during the mahadasha of a benefic the antardasha of an unrelated yogakaraka occasionally gives rajayoga, seems more appropriate to us.

Shlokas 37 and 38 have been explained earlier. There is an important principle enshrined in shloka 39 which says that a maraka, during its mahadasha, does not kill in the antardasha of a related benefic; however, it kills in the antardasha of an unrelated malefic. It means to convey the idea that a maraka dasha would behave badly during the antardasha of even an unrelated malefic; it would certainly kill during the antardasha of its related malefic. The native of chart 19 (JFK), died during the Jupiter-Saturn dasha. Jupiter is a maraka; it did not kill him during its own AD. But it did precipitate the adverse event during the AD of an unrelated malefic Saturn.

Mutual periods of Saturn and Venus

According to our author, Venus and Saturn during their mutual mahadasha-antardasha give the results of each other (shloka 40). This means that during the Venus-Saturn dasha, Saturn would express the results that Venus normally should give depending upon its strength and other dispositions. Similarly, during the Saturn-Venus dasha, Venus should deliver results that Saturn would be expected to deliver according to its dispositions. We have explained these principles with examples. However, there is more to these mutual dasha-antardashas that must be taken note of and not completely rejected. The *Bhavartha Ratnakara* of Sri Ramanuja considers the mutual dasha-antardasha of Venus and Saturn as leading to misfortunes and miseries, except for the lagnas of Jupiter. We did not find this applicable to our example chart (chart 22). On the other hand, the *Uttara Kalamrita* of Kalidas lays certain conditions regarding the mutual dasha-antardashas of these grahas which may not be totally out of place. According to this latter classic, the results of mutual Venus-Saturn dashas are extremely adverse if both the grahas are very strong (exalted, in own house, in moolatrikona, vargottama, etc.). If one of these is weak, the stronger of the two ensures rajayoga results. If both are weak, then too the results are considered to be good.

Mahayogas

The last two shlokas (shlokas 41 and 42) describe two yogas which according to sage Parashara are considered as mahayogas. These involve houses one and ten on the one hand and houses nine and ten on the other. Very potent and benevolent yogas result when the lagna lord and the tenth lord unite together either in the lagna or in the tenth house. Similarly, very potent and benevolent yogas result when the ninth lord and the tenth lord unite in the ninth or the tenth house. If these house lords are not blemished by adverse house lordships, the native earns immense fame and success during his lifetime.

Limitations of the Laghu Parashari

The *Laghu parashari* is a classic which beautifully deals with some of the very fine aspects of interpretation of the Vimshottari dasha. The emphasis of this classic is on identifying the various grades of rajayogas and to work out the manner in which the various dashas would unfold the results of those yogas. Also detailed in this classic are the principles to identify the maraka grahas which would be likely to interrupt the fructification of the yogas when their dashas operate. However, there are several limitations to which this classic is subject, and these limitations must be identified in order to fully take advantage of the great principles enshrined in this classic. This classic does not deal with the several worldly matters which might concern the consulter of an astrologer. Thus such matters as health and disease, marriage, love affairs and relationships, home, children, parents, money matters, legal issues, journeys, spirituality and the like find no mention or guidance in this classic. For all those matters, the student of astrology must use his knowledge garnered from other sources. However, whatever this small classic contains is unrivalled and one should get wonderful results from it as long as one keeps its limitations in mind.

Index

VEDIC ASTROLOGY BOOKS
Dr K S Charak

English Language:

1. Elements of Vedic Astrology (two volumes)
2. Yogas in Astrology
3. Essentials of Medical Astrology
4. Subtleties of Medical Astrology
5. A Textbook of Varshaphala
6. Predictive Techniques in Varshaphala
7. Laghu Jatakam
8. Jatakalankara
9. Surya the Sun God

Hindi Language:

1. Vaidic Jyotish ke Maulika Tattva (two volumes)
2. Chikitsa Jyotish
3. Varshaphala Sarvasva
4. Yoga Mimamsa
5. Jatakalankara

English Language – Author: Rajeev Jhanji

1. Applications of Yogini Dasha
   Editor – Dr K S Charak

Uma Publications
E-mail: vedastrology@yahoo.com

Made in the USA
Coppell, TX
14 February 2024

28997765R00098